River Cottage 2009

Your seasonal guide to the year with a week-to-view diary

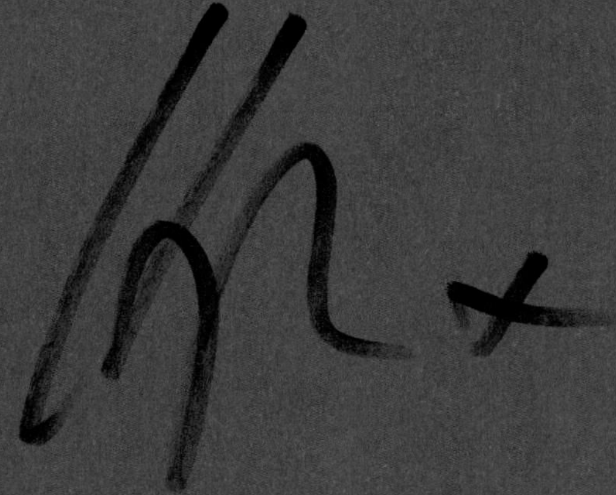

BLOOMSBURY

The River Cottage Team

There's something thrillingly optimistic about a brand new diary. It holds all the excitement of a new year, full of promise and possibilities. I'm certainly very excited at the prospect of this year's diary, as I get to share with you a glimpse of River Cottage HQ during the year. You'll meet many of the exceptional people who work with me every day at Park Farm, as well as some of our experts, such as butcher Ray Smith, and chicken gurus Pammy Riggs and Richard Hicks, from whom I have learned so much since my first days as a smallholder.

New years often start with resolutions to try different things and that's what this year's diary is all about. Each month introduces you to one of our River Cottage experts and the courses they teach here at HQ. Whether you join us for a class or not – and I hope you will – there are lots of tips and advice on getting started yourself. Whether it's keeping bees, raising chickens, making your own jam or baking your own bread – on whatever scale you wish to embrace it, there's infinite satisfaction and scope. Though I'm warning you, trying one thing often leads to tackling another.

At River Cottage, we all have lots of calls on our time. And I'm not kidding anyone – often it's incredibly hard work, but the rewards are enormous. Spending so much time on the farm, in the garden and kitchen ensures that we're always engaged with the seasons. As one thing passes over, there's always something new to look forward to. The end of the game season is softened by knowing spring is just around the corner. Any fleeting sadness I feel as I tuck into the last spear of asparagus dissipates as I contemplate the broad beans, raspberries and tomatoes to come.

There's a soul-feeding pleasure in shaking off the plastic-shrouded shackles of dull consumerism and becoming fully engaged with what you eat and where it comes from. One thing I know for sure is that moving away from industrially produced, large-scale food to something more personal is an infinitely gratifying journey.

So I hope you'll end your year with a deeper knowledge about your food and where it comes from. This diary is a great place to start. Get to know our River Cottage people. Try out some new things, sample one of the 36 recipes and check out the seasonal information, helpful addresses, charts and try-at-home tips. And I hope when December rolls around, your cupboards will be as full as this diary.

All the best,

Hugh

Hugh

River Cottage

Ten years ago, when I moved from London down to Dorset with a dream of raising a few pigs and chickens and being able to fish whenever I wanted, I could hardly have imagined what that dream would become.

In 2006, we moved from the first River Cottage to the larger Park Farm. After what felt like endless searching, we had found our seventeenth-century farmhouse tucked into a beautiful site in the Axe Valley, just outside Axminster, on the borders of Devon and Dorset. With its sixty or so acres of pasture, hedgerows and woodland, we knew we'd found the perfect home for our new River Cottage HQ at Park Farm. Here, we could expand and build for the future.

Today, two years on, the tranquillity of the setting contrasts with the constant activity on the farm. Cattle, sheep, pigs and chickens graze and peck in the fields. Beehives hum by the gorse. The fruit and vegetable gardens provide a constant stream of fresh produce for the kitchen. Hams and salamis hang in the barn to dry and bread is baked in ovens made of clay dragged from the pond.

And our greatest delight is that we get to share our passion for self-sufficiency, food integrity and the consumption of local, seasonal produce with even more people. It's thrilling to see so many of you stroll down the hill to take our classes in everything from foraging, curing, bread and jam making, to butchery and keeping chickens, or to share one of our lively weekend dinners. Our gardening courses have always been popular and we look forward to expanding them this year, to reflect the growing interest we have from city dwellers on the specific challenges and excitement of urban, allotment and climate-change gardening.

We have so many plans for the future and Park Farm promises to be busier than ever in 2009. Keep in touch with what we're up to by subscribing to the River Cottage newsletter at rivercottage.net. And do come and visit us if you can.

Gillon Meller, Ray Smith and Daniel Stevens

Anyone who has enjoyed Park Farm's hospitality owes a debt of thanks to head chef Gillon Meller (see January), chef Daniel Stevens (see February) and Ray Smith (see November), our butchery expert and all around 'meat guru'.

Ray, who has been involved in River Cottage since the beginning, has a warmth and expertise which make him very popular with visitors, and the feeling is reciprocated. Ray often visits people who have been on his courses, taking palpable delight in hams hanging in porches and nettle beer fermenting in kitchens from Aberdeen to Weston-super-Mare.

Gillon was running an organic catering business when he introduced himself to Hugh at a party. A month later, Hugh tracked him down to get him to help out. 'Helping out' became a full-time job and he's been the heart and thoughtful soul of the kitchen for the last four years.

'This is a great place to grow,' Gillon says. 'In a restaurant you wouldn't get the experience of butchery or pick vegetables from your own walled garden. It's a privilege to work with these ingredients. The cooking becomes almost irrelevant, the very last stage in a long process. With the bacon, for example, you've probably fed the pig scraps, and seen the carcass hanging. The last thing is to slice it and cook it but all of the important work's already been done.'

Daniel, too, ended up at River Cottage almost by accident. In 2006, he was given our Pig in a Day course as a present and six months later, he started working as a chef in the kitchen. Daniel is our baking expert, and doesn't mind his frequently singed eyebrows, collateral damage from pulling bread out of the wood-fired oven. 'We always make time for the people who come here and we learn so much from the land team and from Ray. The people here are amazing.'

— *Visit Ray's website at raythemeatguru.com.*

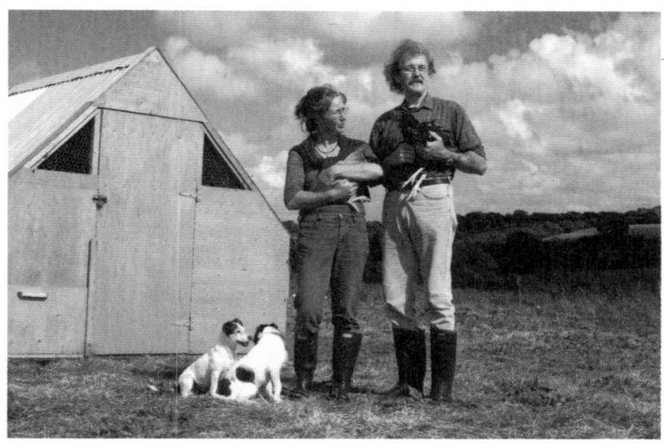

Pammy and Richie Riggs

Within thirty minutes of first meeting, Pammy and Richie Riggs were discussing their shared dream of owning a smallholding. Richie was in the music business and tired of travelling all the time; Pammy was a groom, passionate about country life.

In 1989, they bought seventeen wet Devon acres but it was about as far from an instant happy ending as you can be. Pammy says: 'To get planning permission to build our house we had to prove we could make a living from the land, so in the early years we were living in a caravan with two teenage sons and rearing organic pigs, cattle and sheep. It was tough, but it was what we wanted to do.'

When they started their shop at Providence Farm, Hugh came along to open it and they paid him with a goose and a duck, the first of many chickens, ducks and geese to make their way from their farm to River Cottage.

It was Pammy's extraordinary and calming affinity with poultry that led Hugh to christen her the 'Chicken Whisperer'. These qualities make her a charismatic leader of our All About Chickens course (see April). 'I really enjoy it,' she says. 'I want as many people as possible – in towns as well as the countryside – to start keeping their own birds.'

Farming like this is exhausting, Pammy admits, but she speaks with such passion it's clear she wouldn't live any other way. 'Most people eat like kings on their birthday or at Christmas,' she says. 'We eat like kings every day. We're healthy – we're tired, but we're healthy! All the physical labour keeps you strong. It's what our bodies are meant to do.'

— *Read Pammy's articles on chicken keeping in* Country Smallholding *magazine, a great source of advice, news and tips: countrysmallholding.com.*
— *To find out more about Pammy and Richie, or to order some of their organic pork, beef, lamb or poultry, go to providencefarm.co.uk.*

The Garden Team: Mark Diacono, Victoria Moorey and Emma Stapleforth

'At Park Farm everything slopes down to the kitchen, both literally and metaphorically,' says Mark Diacono (see July), who heads the Garden Team. 'We have a great two-way relationship with the chefs, from plot to plate.'

Emma Stapleforth (see May), who has worked here for two years, agrees. 'For me, the proudest moment is when you bring a perfect box of salad, which you've just picked, into the kitchen and you know everyone is going to really enjoy it.'

Sharing what we do here has always been fundamental, and Mark has big plans for the future. 'If it's grown in England, I want it here. I don't want there to be a taste we can't try, a recipe we can't make, a taste experience we can't share with our visitors.'

Our newest recruit is Victoria Moorey, who swapped a career in the motor industry for a two-acre smallholding and a job as a gardening assistant at Park Farm. 'Years ago, my husband and I came on a Catch and Cook course, so I know just how people feel when they come here. Sometimes visitors say to me, "I'd love to live like this but I never could," and I say never say never! We thought that and look at me now. If it's what you really want to do, I say do it!'

— *Garden Organic (Henry Doubleday Research Association), gardenorganic.org.uk, for information on organic gardening.*
— *Biodynamic Agricultural Association, biodynamic.org.uk, for information on gardening biodynamically.*

Liz Neville and Pam Corbin

Visitors couldn't be in safer hands on Preserves days. Pam Corbin and Liz Neville start early, rattling down the hill to Park Farm at 7.30 a.m., their cars packed full of preserving pans, jars and wooden spoons, ready to transform heaps of fresh produce into a satisfying stash of jams, jellies, chutneys, curds and cordials.

For many years, 'Pam the Jam' (see September) ran her own preserves company, Thursday Cottage, and Liz, maker of our famous River Cottage Glutney, still makes jams and chutneys under her Parrett Preserve label in a converted cowshed next to her home.

Liz worked in a bank for thirty-five years when what was once a hobby became her job. 'I met Hugh when he opened our local village show and he bought my chutney and some of my raspberry and rhubarb jam,' explains Liz. 'Then he tracked me down to find out if I'd like to make jam and chutney for River Cottage.'

The two women radiate cheerfulness, though they confess to having slightly different techniques with certain things. This, Pam says, 'makes for lively days full of banter!' 'But we know what we're doing, we've been doing it for so long. It's like your times tables, it just comes out automatically,' says Liz, the former bank worker.

— River Cottage Handbook No.2: Preserves *by Pam Corbin, Bloomsbury, £12.99.*
— *Brogdale is home of the National Fruit Collection, the largest collection of its kind in the world. The website, brogdale.org, is a good source of information on many fruit varieties.*

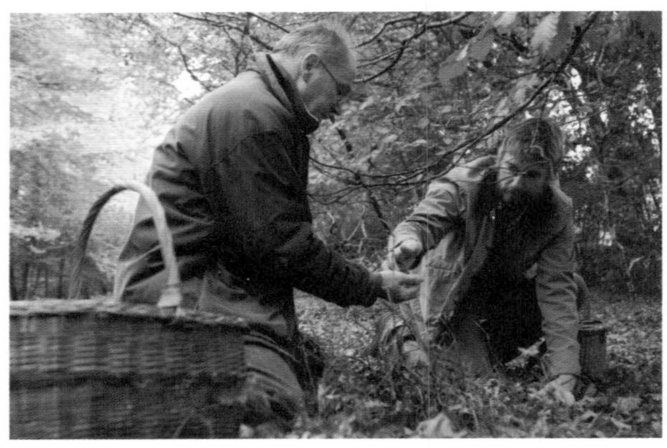

John Wright and Steven Lamb

There are few activities that make you feel more deeply rooted in the seasons than foraging. Mancunian Steven Lamb (see October), resident host for many River Cottage events was, until five years ago, a confirmed urbanite. Today, he feels a genuine thrill at the first brisk chill that might herald autumn and the beginning of the mushroom season.

Like many at River Cottage, Steve puts his new-found passion for foraging down to his friendship with John Wright (see June), our wild food expert. Says Steve, 'John has so much knowledge and yet he wears it so lightly and imparts it with so much humour, so much generosity, it's hard to resist. John is a translator, shedding light on to the world around us, particularly the free larder of the countryside.'

John has been wild about mushrooms since he was fourteen. A cabinet-maker by trade, his love of foraging was rekindled in earnest when he moved to Dorset in the early 1980s and spent every spare moment in the countryside, his Richard Mabey *Food for Free* book in one hand and a basket in the other.

John has worked with us at River Cottage for eight years, leading the Mushroom Hunts and Edible Seashore days. He loves to share all he knows. 'I like seeing people's eyes light up, and they really do. Seeing grown people paddling in rock pools, it takes them back to their childhoods. When you go for a walk, it's all about you, but when you go for a forage it's all about the quarry, it takes you out of yourself, forces you to really look and be still. So many people say to me, "That's the best day I've had in ages … ".'

— River Cottage Handbook No.1: Mushrooms *by John Wright, Bloomsbury, £12.99.*
— *Visit John's own website at mushroomhunting.co.uk.*

Personal notes

Name

Home address

Telephone

Fax

Mobile

Email

Work address

Telephone

Fax

Mobile

Email

Emergency contact

Address

Telephone

Fax

Mobile

Email

Conversion charts

Useful measurements

Measurement	Imperial	Metric
1 American cup	8fl oz	225ml
1 egg, size 3	2fl oz	56ml
1 egg white	1fl oz	28ml
1 rounded tablespoon flour	1oz	30g
1 rounded tablespoon cornflour	1oz	30g
1 rounded tablespoon caster sugar	1oz	30g
2 rounded tablespoons fresh breadcrumbs	1oz	30g
2 level teaspoons gelatine	¼oz	8g
1 American tablespoon of butter	½oz	15g
packet granular aspic	1oz sets 1 pint liquid	30g sets 570ml liquid
3 leaves powdered gelatine	½oz sets 1 pint liquid	15g sets 570ml liquid

Volumes

Imperial	Metric
1 tsp	5ml
2 tbsp	28ml
4 tbsp	56ml
2fl oz	55ml
3fl oz	75ml
5fl oz (¼ pint)	150ml
6.6fl oz (⅓ pint)	190ml
10fl oz (½ pint)	290ml
15fl oz (¾ pint)	425ml
20fl oz (1 pint)	570ml
35fl oz (1¾ pints)	1 litre

Wine quantities

	fl oz	ml
1 glass liqueur	1	45
1 glass port/sherry	2	70
1 glass wine	3	100
average wine bottle	25	750

Oven temperatures

°C	°F	Gas
140	275	1
150	300	2
170	325	3
180	350	4
190	375	5
200	400	6
220	425	7
230	450	8
240	475	9

Weights

Imperial	Metric
¼oz	7–8g
½oz	15g
¾oz	20g
1oz	30g
2oz	55g
3oz	85g
4oz (¼lb)	110g
5oz	140g
6oz	170g
7oz	200g
8oz (½lb)	225g
9oz	255g
10oz	285g
11oz	310g
12oz (¾lb)	340g
13oz	370g
14oz	400g
15oz	425g
16oz (1lb)	450g
1¼lb	560g
1½lb	675g
2lb	900g
3lb	1.35kg
4lb	1.8kg
5lb	2.3kg
6lb	2.7kg
7lb	3.2kg
8lb	3.6kg
9lb	4kg
10lb	4.5kg

For fan-assisted ovens reduce temperature by 20°C.

Measurements

Imperial	Metric
1/16in	2mm
1/12in	3mm
⅛in	4mm
¼in	6mm
½in	1cm
¾in	2cm
1in	2.5cm
1¼in	3cm
1½in	4cm
1¾in	4.5cm
2in	5cm
2½in	6cm
3in	7.5cm
3½in	9cm
4in	10cm
5in	13cm
5¼in	13.5cm
6in	15cm
6½in	16cm
7in	18cm
7½in	19cm
8in	20cm
9in	23cm
9½in	24cm
10in	25.5cm
11in	28cm
12in	30cm
13in	32.5cm
14in	35cm
16in	40cm

Shooting seasons

Game and wild fowl

Coot	1 Sept–31 Jan
Duck and goose	
inland England, Scotland, Wales	1 Sept–31 Jan
foreshore England, Scotland, Wales	1 Sept–20 Feb
N. Ireland	1 Sept–31 Jan
Golden plover	1 Sept–31 Jan
Grouse	
England, Scotland, Wales	12 Aug–10 Dec
N. Ireland	12 Aug–30 Nov
Hare	
England, Scotland, Wales	cannot be sold 1 March–31 July
N. Ireland	12 Aug–31 Jan
Moorhen	1 Sept–31 Jan
Partridge	1 Sept–1 Feb
Pheasant	
England, Scotland, Wales	1 Oct–1 Feb
N. Ireland (cocks only)	1 Oct–31 Jan
Rabbit	no closed season
Common snipe	
England, Scotland, Wales	12 Aug–31 Jan
N. Ireland	1 Sept–31 Jan
Jack snipe (N. Ireland only)	1 Sept–31 Jan
Woodcock	
England, Wales	1 Oct–31 Jan
Scotland	1 Sept–31 Jan
Wood pigeon	no closed season

Deer

Fallow buck	1 Aug–30 Apr
Fallow doe	
England, Wales, N. Ireland	1 Nov–28 Feb
Scotland	21 Oct–15 Feb
Red deer stag	
England, Wales, N. Ireland	1 Aug–30 Apr
Scotland	1 July–20 Oct
Red deer hind	
England, Wales, N. Ireland	1 Nov–28 Feb
Scotland	21 Oct–15 Feb
Roe buck	
England, Wales	1 Apr–31 Oct
Scotland	1 Apr–20 Oct
Roe doe	
England, Wales	1 Nov–28 Feb
Scotland	21 Oct–31 Mar
Sika stag	
England, Wales, N. Ireland	1 Aug–30 Apr
Scotland	1 July–20 Oct
Sika hind	
England, Wales, N. Ireland	1 Nov–28 Feb
Scotland	21 Oct–15 Feb

Landing sizes

Bass	360mm
Black sea bream	230mm
Brill	300mm
Clam	40mm
Razor clam	100mm
Cockles	23mm
Cod	350mm
Conger eel	580mm
Brown crab	140mm
Spider crab	
female	120mm
male	130mm
Velvet crab	65mm
Crawfish	110mm
Dab	230mm
Flounder	270mm
Haddock	300mm
Hake	270mm
Herring	200mm
Lemon sole	250mm
Ling	630mm
Blue ling	700mm
Lobster	87mm
Mackerel	300mm
Megrim	200mm
Grey mullet	300mm
Mussel	50mm
Oyster	70mm
Plaice	270mm
Pollack	300mm
Queen scallop	40mm
Red mullet	150mm
Red sea bream	250mm
Saithe	350mm
Horse mackerel scad	250mm
Scallops	110mm
Whole skate	400mm
Wing skate	200mm
Sole	240mm
Sardine	110mm
Turbot	300mm
Whelk	45mm
Whiting	270mm

These charts are to be used as a guide and should not be used as a definitive statement of current regulations.

Sowing and planting times for vegetables

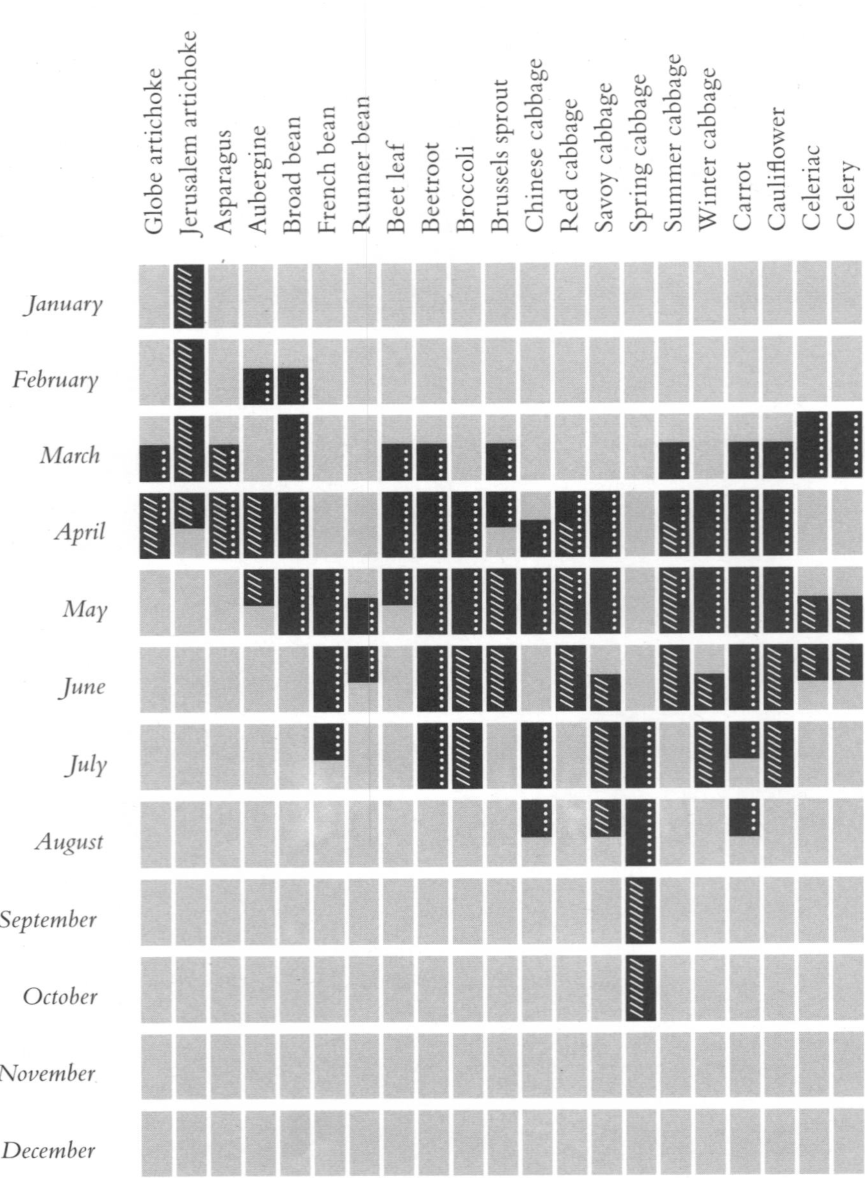

Cucumber

Kale

Leek

Early winter crop lettuce

Spring crop lettuce

Summer crop lettuce

Mangetout and petit pois

Marrow

Onion and shallot from sets

Onion from seed

Parsnip

Pea (June/July crop)

Pea (August crop)

Pea (Autumn Crop)

Asparagus pea

Potato

Radish

Rhubarb

Spinach

Swede

Greenhouse tomato

 *Plant*

 *Sow*

Planting times for fruit

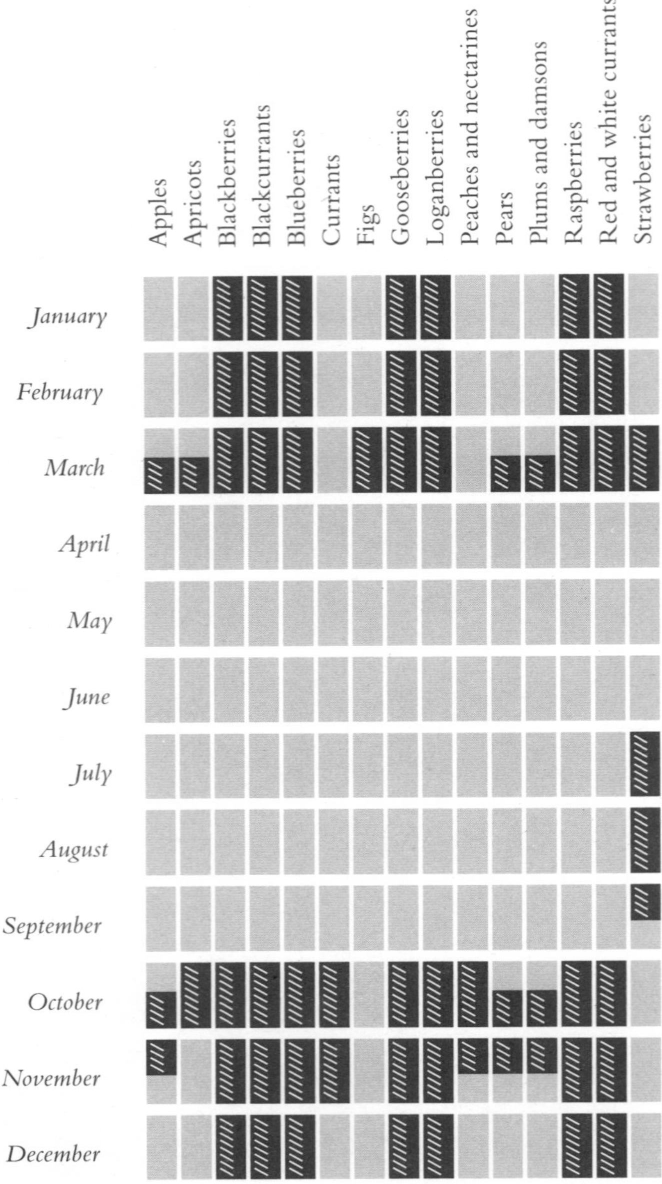

Plant

Sowing and planting times for herbs

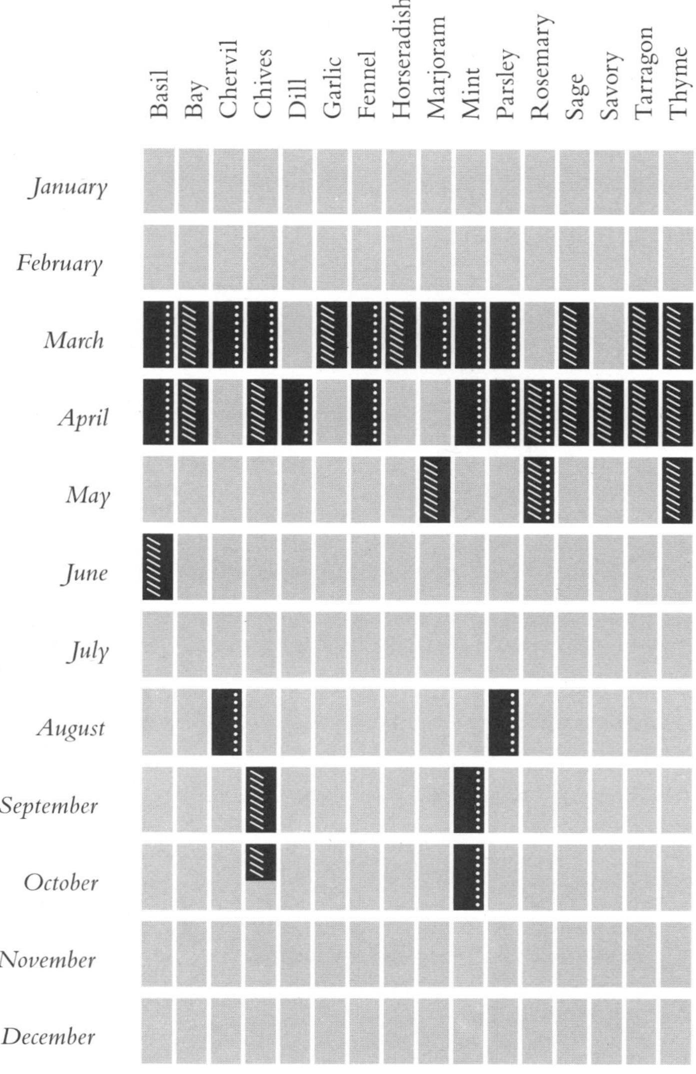

Useful websites

actionaid.org Action Aid. An agency whose aim is to fight poverty worldwide.

aonb.org.uk Offers general information about Areas of Outstanding Natural Beauty (AONBs) in England, Wales and Northern Ireland.

asao.co.uk Association of Show and Agricultural Organisations. The full listing of all agricultural shows across the UK.

basc.org.uk British Association for Shooting and Conservation. Aims to encourage the development of country shooting and adherence to codes of practice.

bigbarn.co.uk A one-stop site where you can find your local food producers and buy direct.

biodynamic.org.uk Biodynamic Agricultural Association. Promotes and supports a biodynamic approach to farming, forestry and gardening. Details of biodynamic events and courses.

cat.org.uk Centre for Alternative Technology. Recommends practical solutions to environmental problems for the twenty-first century.

chickenout.tv Chicken Out. Our campaign for higher welfare conditions for chickens farmed in the UK.

ciwf.org.uk Compassion in World Farming. Aims to bring an end to factory farming and the long-distance transport of animals worldwide.

countrysmallholding.com Useful information for smallholders, poultry keepers and organic gardeners. Includes advice on keeping chickens, a breeders' directory and the opportunity to send questions to qualified vets.

defra.gov.uk Department for Environment, Food and Rural Affairs. Advice on all aspects of farming and farm regulations. Cattle registration forms can be downloaded from the website.

energysavingtrust.org.uk Energy Saving Trust. Find out more about saving energy, money and the environment in your home.

fairtrade.org.uk Fairtrade Foundation. Guarantees a better deal for producers in developing countries. Over one hundred products now carry a Fairtrade logo and the website tells you where to find them, as well as what you can do to support Fairtrade.

farma.org.uk National Farmers' Retail & Markets Association. The largest organisation of its type in the world, representing direct sales to customers through farm shops, pick-your-own, farmers' markets, home delivery, on-farm catering, and farm entertainment throughout the UK.

fishing.co.uk Information about sea and land fishing.

foe.co.uk Friends of the Earth. International network of environmental pressure groups, with a string of local groups in the UK.

foodfrombritain.com Food From Britain. Regional food and drink guide; list of over 4,000 UK producers and regional events.

freerangereview.com Free Range Review. Details of the very best produce in your area. You can join your local food community to discover, review, add and discuss your favourite foodie places.

fwag.org.uk Farming & Wildlife Advisory Group. Exists to provide farmers, landowners and other clients with the best opportunity for environmental gain through cost-effective, quality solutions.

gametoeat.co.uk Game to Eat. All you need to know about game, including suppliers, recipes and useful links.

gct.org.uk The Game & Wildlife Conservation Trust. Promotes the conservation of game in the British countryside and advises on practical management techniques.

greenpeace.org.uk Greenpeace. Campaigns on environmental issues.

guildofqbutchers.com Guild of Q Butchers. A useful contact if you are looking for specialist butchers in your area.

localfoods.org.uk Local Foods. Maps of farmers' markets, farm shops and information on obtaining other local foods direct from the producer.

metoffice.co.uk The Met Office. Detailed weather forecasts and inshore waters forecast.

naturalengland.org.uk Natural England (was English Nature). Offers advice and information on the conservation of wildlife and natural features throughout England.

rare-breeds.com Rare Breeds Survival Trust. Charity aiming to conserve Britain's native livestock heritage. Offers details of rare-breed meat suppliers in your area.

rivercottage.net A website set up to encourage discussion about food, where it comes from and why that matters. Includes edible projects, recipes and recommended producers.

savetodaysavetomorrow.com A website that offers advice on how to make your home more sustainable and reduce your carbon footprint.

slowfood.org.uk Slow Food. An Italian-based international organisation of 'eco-gastronomes' wishing to preserve artisan foods and regional traditions.

soilassociation.org The Soil Association. Offers support and advice on growing and producing organic food.

2009

January

M	T	W	T	F	**S**	**S**
			1	2	**3**	**4**
5	6	7	8	9	**10**	**11**
12	13	14	15	16	**17**	**18**
19	20	21	22	23	**24**	**25**
26	27	28	29	30	**31**	

February

M	T	W	T	F	**S**	**S**
						1
2	3	4	5	6	**7**	**8**
9	10	11	12	13	**14**	**15**
16	17	18	19	20	**21**	**22**
23	24	25	26	27	**28**	

March

M	T	W	T	F	**S**	**S**
						1
2	3	4	5	6	**7**	**8**
9	10	11	12	13	**14**	**15**
16	17	18	19	20	**21**	**22**
23	24	25	26	27	**28**	**29**
30	31					

April

M	T	W	T	F	**S**	**S**
		1	2	3	**4**	**5**
6	7	8	9	**10**	**11**	**12**
13	14	15	16	17	**18**	**19**
20	21	22	23	24	**25**	**26**
27	28	29	30			

May

M	T	W	T	F	**S**	**S**
				1	**2**	**3**
4	5	6	7	8	**9**	**10**
11	12	13	14	15	**16**	**17**
18	19	20	21	22	**23**	**24**
25	26	27	28	29	**30**	**31**

June

M	T	W	T	F	**S**	**S**
1	2	3	4	5	**6**	**7**
8	9	10	11	12	**13**	**14**
15	16	17	18	19	**20**	**21**
22	23	24	25	26	**27**	**28**
29	30					

July

M	T	W	T	F	**S**	**S**
		1	2	3	**4**	**5**
6	7	8	9	10	**11**	**12**
13	14	15	16	17	**18**	**19**
20	21	22	23	24	**25**	**26**
27	28	29	30	31		

August

M	T	W	T	F	**S**	**S**
					1	**2**
3	4	5	6	7	**8**	**9**
10	11	12	13	14	**15**	**16**
17	18	19	20	21	**22**	**23**
24	25	26	27	28	**29**	**30**
31						

September

M	T	W	T	F	**S**	**S**
	1	2	3	4	**5**	**6**
7	8	9	10	11	**12**	**13**
14	15	16	17	18	**19**	**20**
21	22	23	24	25	**26**	**27**
28	29	30				

October

M	T	W	T	F	**S**	**S**
			1	2	**3**	**4**
5	6	7	8	9	**10**	**11**
12	13	14	15	16	**17**	**18**
19	20	21	22	23	**24**	**25**
26	27	28	29	30	**31**	

November

M	T	W	T	F	**S**	**S**
						1
2	3	4	5	6	**7**	**8**
9	10	11	12	13	**14**	**15**
16	17	18	19	20	**21**	**22**
23	24	25	26	27	**28**	**29**
30						

December

M	T	W	T	F	**S**	**S**
	1	2	3	4	**5**	**6**
7	8	9	10	11	**12**	**13**
14	15	16	17	18	**19**	**20**
21	22	23	24	**25**	**26**	**27**
28	29	30	31			

2010

January

M	T	W	T	F	S	S
				1	2	3
4	5	6	7	8	9	10
11	12	13	14	15	16	17
18	19	20	21	22	23	24
25	26	27	28	29	30	31

February

M	T	W	T	F	S	S
1	2	3	4	5	6	7
8	9	10	11	12	13	14
15	16	17	18	19	20	21
22	23	24	25	26	27	28

March

M	T	W	T	F	S	S
1	2	3	4	5	6	7
8	9	10	11	12	13	14
15	16	17	18	19	20	21
22	23	24	25	26	27	28
29	30	31				

April

M	T	W	T	F	S	S
			1	2	3	4
5	6	7	8	9	10	11
12	13	14	15	16	17	18
19	20	21	22	23	24	25
26	27	28	29	30		

May

M	T	W	T	F	S	S
					1	2
3	4	5	6	7	8	9
10	11	12	13	14	15	16
17	18	19	20	21	22	23
24	25	26	27	28	29	30
31						

June

M	T	W	T	F	S	S
	1	2	3	4	5	6
7	8	9	10	11	12	13
14	15	16	17	18	19	20
21	22	23	24	25	26	27
28	29	30				

July

M	T	W	T	F	S	S
			1	2	3	4
5	6	7	8	9	10	11
12	13	14	15	16	17	18
19	20	21	22	23	24	25
26	27	28	29	30	31	

August

M	T	W	T	F	S	S
						1
2	3	4	5	6	7	8
9	10	11	12	13	14	15
16	17	18	19	20	21	22
23	24	25	26	27	28	29
30	31					

September

M	T	W	T	F	S	S
		1	2	3	4	5
6	7	8	9	10	11	12
13	14	15	16	17	18	19
20	21	22	23	24	25	26
27	28	29	30			

October

M	T	W	T	F	S	S
				1	2	3
4	5	6	7	8	9	10
11	12	13	14	15	16	17
18	19	20	21	22	23	24
25	26	27	28	29	30	31

November

M	T	W	T	F	S	S
1	2	3	4	5	6	7
8	9	10	11	12	13	14
15	16	17	18	19	20	21
22	23	24	25	26	27	28
29	30					

December

M	T	W	T	F	S	S
		1	2	3	4	5
6	7	8	9	10	11	12
13	14	15	16	17	18	19
20	21	22	23	24	25	26
27	28	29	30	31		

29 Monday

30 Tuesday

31 Wednesday

1 Thursday

New Year's Day (bank holiday)

January

Game in a day
Gillon Meller

Wander down the hill to Park Farm on a game day and expect fur and feathers to fly. As you approach the farm, a host of pheasant, partridge and rabbits hang in the barn and in the dining room, a whole fallow or sika deer, still in its fur, waits for butcher Ray Smith to break down the carcass into its cuts. Head chef, Gillon Meller, steps in to share his passion for game and the many ways you can prepare it. He dresses a haunch to roast for lunch and, while it's cooking, gets on with the seriously delicious business of making venison haggis and sausages.

There's no time to slack in the afternoon, as visitors prepare red-leg partridges for the oven, skin and joint rabbits to transform them into a tasty stew and learn how to hot smoke pheasant breasts.

Getting started

— Try as big a variety of game as you can, simply prepared, so you can work out what you like and how long you like it hung for.

— Buy what you can still in its fur or feathers to practise plucking game birds and skinning rabbits.

— If at all possible, go to a farm or a managed estate shoot and befriend the gamekeeper or estate manager – it's the best, freshest and most economical way to buy game.

Contacts

— To buy game online, try the Wild Meat Company, wildmeat.co.uk, or Somerset Organics, somersetorganics.co.uk.

What's good in January

Vegetables *Jerusalem artichokes, Brussels sprouts, Brussels tops, cabbages (red, white and various green varieties), Celery, Chicory, Endive, Greens (spring and winter), Kale (and Borecole), Leeks, Lettuces, Onions, Parsnips, Potatoes, Swedes* ***Fruit*** *Pears, late (Concorde, Doyenne du Comice, Conference, Winter Nellis), Rhubarb (forced)* ***Fungi & Nuts*** *Chestnuts* ***Fish & shellfish*** *Cockles, Cod, Crabs (brown, cock and hen), Oysters (rock), Whiting* ***Game*** *Hare, Partridge, Pheasant, Snipe, Woodcock*

Venison steak au poivre

Season *4 noisettes of venison* (taken from the loin) with *salt and black pepper*. Melt *a knob of butter* in a large, heavy frying pan with *1 tbsp oil*. Fry the noisettes for just over a minute on each side for medium rare. Put the steaks on to a warmed plate and let them rest for a few minutes – don't wash the pan. Put the pan back over a medium-high heat and add *2 tbsp pickled green peppercorns*, drained. Use the back of a wooden spoon to crush them slightly, then add *50ml brandy*, stirring to scrape all of the brown bits off the bottom of the pan and letting the brandy reduce for a minute. Add *200ml double cream* and any juices from the resting steaks, stir and cook for a minute or so to thicken. Taste and adjust the seasoning if necessary and serve, poured over the steaks, with creamy mash. *Serves 2–4.*

Pot roast pheasant with chorizo, butter beans and parsley

Preheat the oven to 170°C/Gas Mark 3. Place a large casserole over a medium heat, and warm *a knob of butter* and *1 tbsp olive oil*. Add *2 finely sliced onions*, *4 finely sliced garlic cloves*, *4 sprigs of thyme* and *2 bay leaves*. Cook for 10 minutes until soft and golden. Meanwhile, set a large frying pan over a high heat and add *2 tbsp olive oil*. Season *2 oven-ready pheasants* with *salt and black pepper*, brown on all sides for 3–4 minutes and transfer to the casserole. Add *300g cooking chorizo*, skin removed and cut into 3cm chunks, to the frying pan and fry for 3–4 minutes to brown, then add to the casserole. Deglaze the frying pan with some *white wine*, then add to the casserole, along with a further *300ml wine*, *500ml chicken stock* and a *400g tin of butter beans*, drained and rinsed. Bring to a simmer, cover and place in the oven for 2 hours. Remove the birds and rest in a warm place. If the chorizo has released a lot of fat, skim some off. Add a handful of *chopped flat-leaf parsley* to the casserole and season. Carve the birds and divide them between warmed plates. Spoon over the chorizo, beans and sauce, and serve with mash or bread. *Serves 4.*

Rabbit satay with spicy peanut sauce

Mix together *1½ tbsp grated fresh ginger*, *2 finely chopped red or green chillies*, *2 crushed garlic cloves*, *half a small onion, grated*, *2 tsp crushed coriander seeds*, *2 tbsp dark soy sauce*, *1 tbsp brown sugar* and the *juice of half a lime*. Add about *600g cubed rabbit meat* from the saddle and back legs and leave to marinate in the fridge for a couple of hours. Soak *10 bamboo skewers* in water for at least 30 minutes. To make the sauce, gently sauté *a finely chopped onion* and *2 crushed garlic cloves* in *1 tbsp groundnut oil* until soft and lightly browned. Add *½–1 finely chopped fresh red or green chilli*, *2–3 tbsp dark soy sauce*, *1 tbsp brown sugar*, *125g crunchy peanut butter* and the *juice of ½–1 lime* and mix well. Let it bubble and thicken in the pan. Taste and add more lime juice, chilli or soy, according to your preference, and a little water to get a 'pourable-but-only-just' consistency. Thread 5 or 6 pieces of meat on each skewer. Cook on a barbecue or a lightly oiled heavy griddle pan or hotplate, turning regularly, until nicely browned, about 10 minutes. Serve with the sauce. *Makes 10 skewers.*

Pot roast pheasant with chorizo, butter beans and parsley

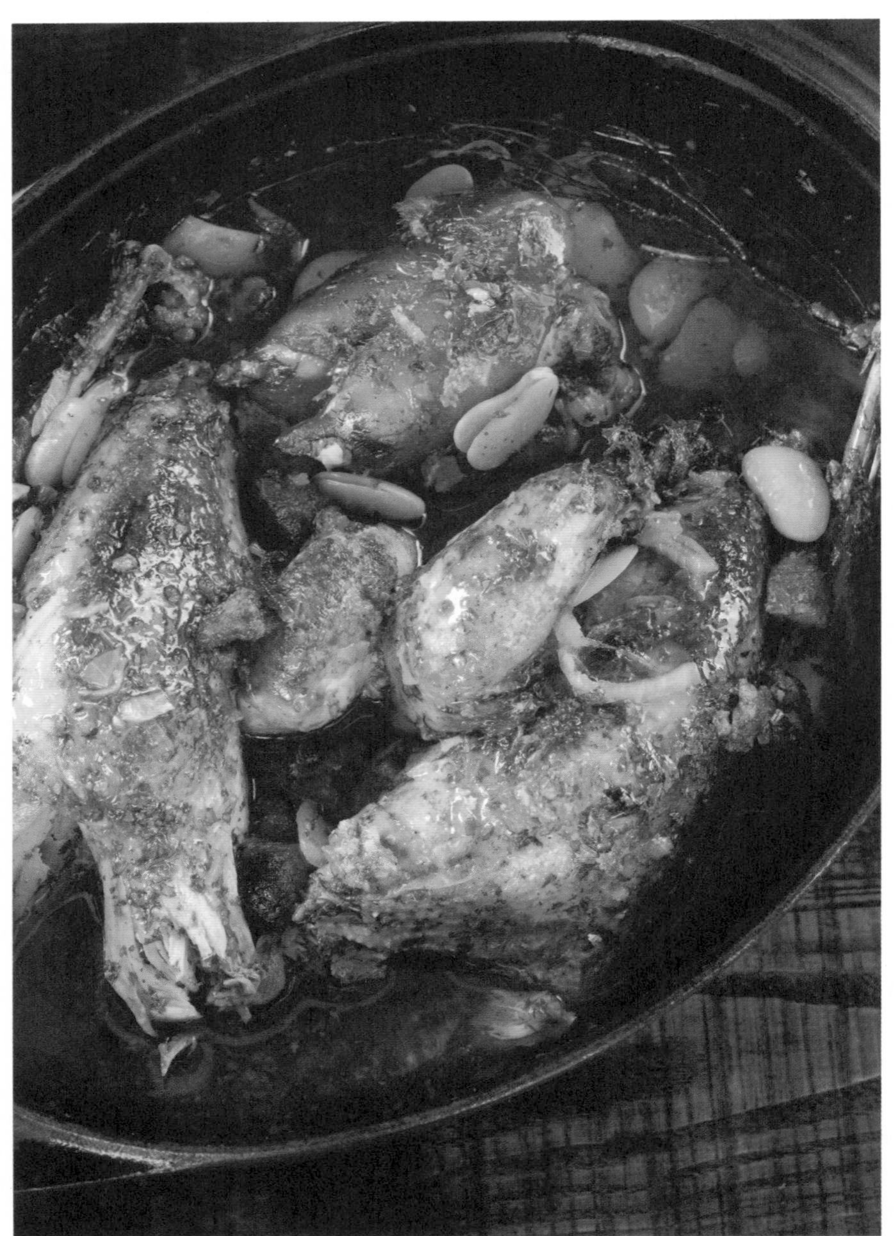

Friday

2

Bank Holiday (Scotland)

Saturday

3

Sunday ◐

4

Notes

January

5 Monday

6 Tuesday

7 Wednesday

8 Thursday

Friday

9

Saturday

10

Bridport Farmers' Market

Sunday ○

11

Notes

January

12 Monday

13 Tuesday

14 Wednesday

15 Thursday

Friday **16**

Saturday **17**

Sunday ◑ **18**

Notes ***January***

19 Monday

20 Tuesday

21 Wednesday

22 Thursday

Friday

23

Saturday

24

Sunday

25

Farmhouse Breakfast Week (farmhousebreakfast.com), until Saturday 31 January
Burns night

Notes

January

26

● Monday

Farmhouse Breakfast Week continues until Saturday 31 January

27

Tuesday

28

Wednesday

29

Thursday

February

Build and bake
Daniel Stevens

At River Cottage in February, wellies and waterproofs are usually the order of the day, particularly if you're joining us for one of our Build and Bake courses. Once visitors have finished pounding the clay for the oven, they get to pummel the dough for the bread, so it's a workout guaranteed to banish any winter sluggishness.

The day begins on the banks of the pond, digging out clay to form the bricks for the igloo-shaped oven. Everyone pitches in with the satisfyingly muddy business of building the first layer so that when visitors go home, they know exactly how to create an oven in their own garden.

Next, it's off to the warmth of the kitchen where chef Daniel Stevens shares his love of baking and demonstrates the art of the loaf. He begins with white bread and a spelt or wholemeal loaf and then moves on to the very important task of making the perfect pizza. Visitors roll out their own bases, and throw on their own toppings before putting them in the clay oven in time for lunch.

Getting started

— Daniel recommends trying the same recipe with a variety of flours to get to know their characteristics – the difference between one flour and another can be remarkable.

— You may think a plain white loaf is the easiest place to start, but Daniel recommends starting with a wholemeal or multigrain loaf. 'They're much more forgiving for a beginner,' he says.

— To learn more about baking bread, check out *River Cottage Handbook No.3: Bread* by Daniel Stevens, Bloomsbury, £12.99.

Contacts

— Great bread starts with good flour. Dove's Farm, dovesfarm.co.uk, and Shipton Mill, shipton-mill.com, both have large ranges and are widely available. If you're in the West Country, look out for Stoates' Flour from Cann Mills in Shaftesbury, stoatesflour.co.uk.

What's good in February

Vegetables *Jerusalem artichokes, Brussels sprouts, Brussels tops, cabbages (red, white and various green varieties), Chicory, Endive, Greens (spring and winter), Kale (and Borecole), Leeks, Lettuces, Onions, Potatoes, Swedes* ***Fruit*** *Rhubarb (forced)* ***Fish & shellfish*** *Cockles, Cod, Crabs (brown, cock and hen), Oysters (rock)* ***Game*** *Hare*

Honey and walnut soda bread

Preheat the oven to 200°C/Gas Mark 6 and lightly oil a baking sheet. Divide *200g shelled walnuts* into two roughly equal piles. Put one half into a food processor or a mortar and crush to a coarse powder. Using your hands, break the other pile of walnuts into large, rough chunks. Put *200g honey* in a pan with *300ml water* and heat gently until the honey dissolves. Cool slightly. Put *500g wholemeal flour, 4 tsp baking powder, 10g salt* and all the walnuts in a large bowl and combine. Pour in the honey water and mix to a soft dough. Turn the dough out on to a lightly floured surface, shape it into a rough, round loaf and place on the oiled baking tray. Slice a deep cross into the top, going almost right the way through to the baking sheet. Bake for 30–35 minutes, until well risen and golden brown. Remove, set aside to cool and serve immediately – at the very latest, eat within 24 hours. *Serves 6.*

Flatbreads

Sift *250g plain flour* into a mixing bowl with *1 tsp salt*. Stir *1 tbsp olive oil* into *150ml warm water*. Pour the liquid over the flour in a thin stream, stirring all the time, until you have a soft mass of slightly sticky dough. Turn the dough out on to a lightly floured work surface and knead until the dough feels smooth and plump, about 5 minutes. Cover the ball of dough with the upturned mixing bowl and let it rest for at least 15 minutes. Divide the dough into 8 pieces and roll each one into a ball. Flour the work surface and a rolling pin and roll out each ball into a round roughly the size of a small plate. Heat a frying pan over a high heat and when it's good and hot, turn the heat down to low. Shake off any excess flour and carefully lay a flatbread in the pan. Let it sit for between 30 seconds and a minute, until you see little white spots forming on the surface, then flip it over. Cook the other side for another 30 seconds. Wrap each cooked flatbread in a tea towel to keep warm and soft while you cook the rest. Serve immediately. *Makes about 8.*

Eggy bread

Cut the crusts off *2–4 slices good white bread*. You can either use whole slices or cut them into fat fingers. Break *2 free-range eggs* into a shallow dish. Add *1 tbsp caster sugar* and beat well with a fork. Lay the bread slices in the eggy mixture, turning them over and letting them sit in the bowl for about 5 minutes so that the egg really soaks in. Heat a frying pan over a medium heat and pour in *1 tbsp sunflower oil*. As soon as the oil is hot, carefully place the eggy bread slices in the pan. After about a minute, the slices should have turned golden brown underneath, so flip them over and cook the other side. When they're done, lift them out of the pan and put them on a warm plate. Serve immediately with *dollops of jam or honey* and a dusting of *icing sugar* if you like. *Serves 2.*

Eggy bread

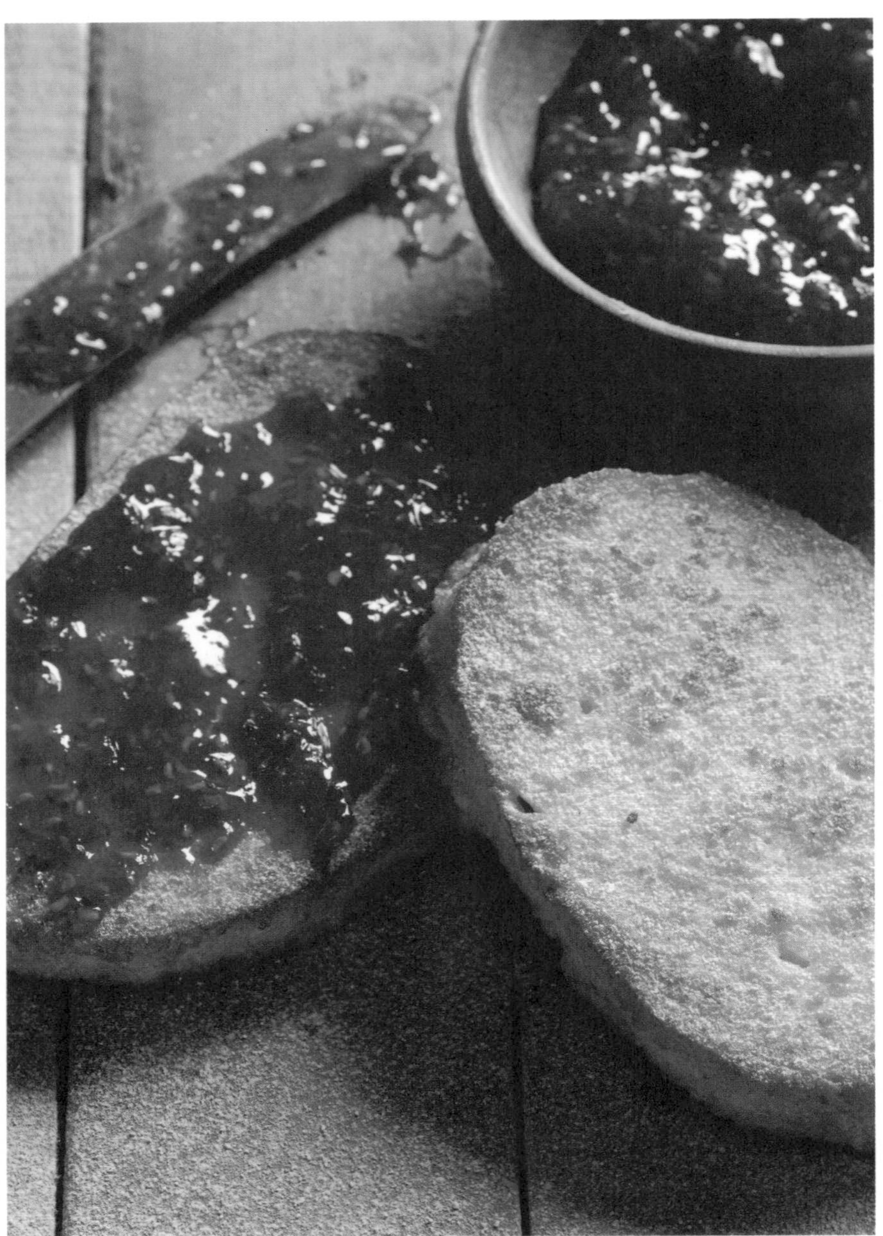

Friday

30

Farmhouse Breakfast Week continues until Saturday 31 January

Saturday

31

Sunday

1

Notes

February

2 ◐ Monday

3 Tuesday

4 Wednesday

5 Thursday

Friday **6**

Saturday **7**

Sunday **8**

Notes ***February***

9 ○ Monday

10 Tuesday

11 Wednesday

12 Thursday

Friday

13

Saturday

14

Bridport Farmers' Market
St Valentine's Day

Sunday

15

Notes

February

16 ◑ Monday

17 Tuesday

18 Wednesday

19 Thursday

Friday

20

Saturday

21

Sunday

22

Notes

February

23 Monday

24 Tuesday

Shrove Tuesday (Pancake Day)

25 ● Wednesday

Ash Wednesday

26 Thursday

March

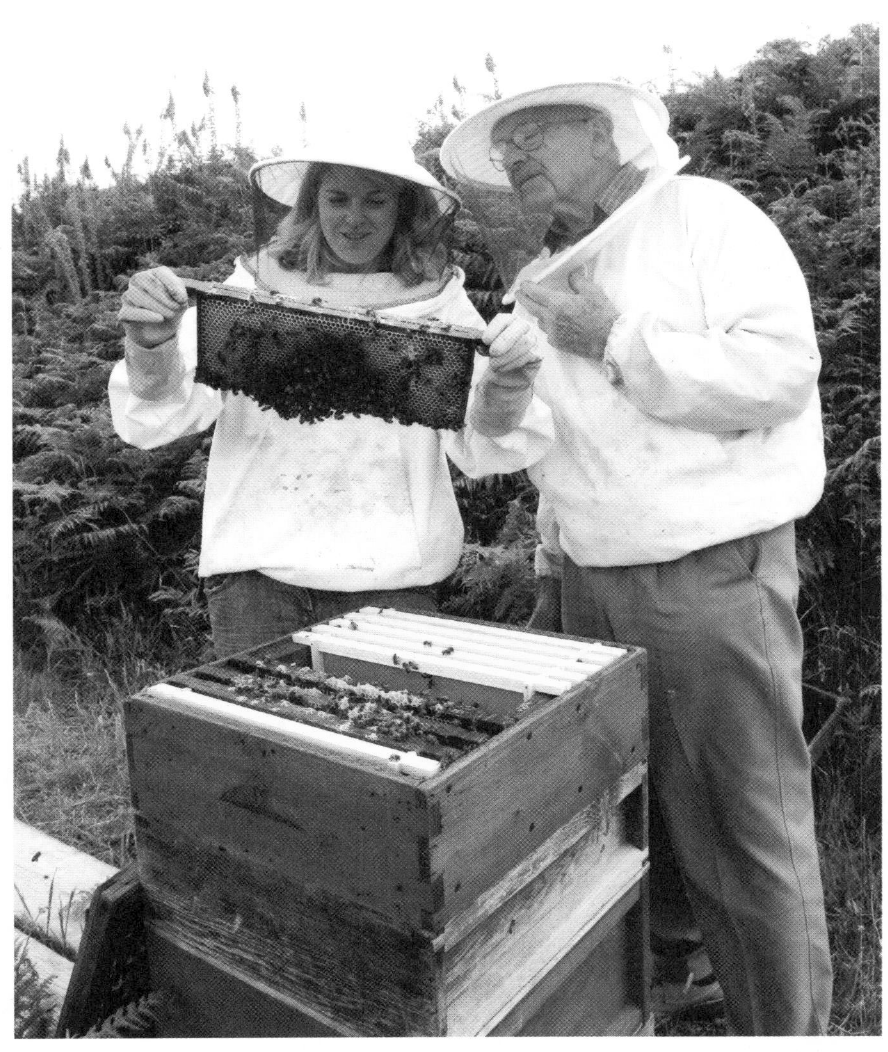

Bees
Cat Streatfeild and Dave Wiscombe

For visitors attending our Introduction to Beekeeping day, the first sight of a real, live, buzzing hive sometimes comes as a bit of a shock. Dave Wiscombe, who leads the course with Cat Streatfeild, has been keeping bees for almost fifty years. He explains, 'It's often a big surprise for people who've only seen bees in books to be confronted with 50,000 of them at once!'

After Dave's introductory talk, visitors dress up in their bee suits and veils and head up the hill to see our three hives huddled in the middle of the gorse. Fear gives way to fascination as our would-be-beekeepers grow more comfortable working with the hives, learning how to handle the bees safely and recognising the different stages of their life cycle. And, as Dave explains, it's not all about the honey – though that's certainly the star attraction – the bounty of beeswax for polish and candles, and the possibility of mead, can cut through the reserve of the most timid of apiarists.

Getting started

— Joining your local beekeeping association is an absolute must. It's a source of advice, guidance and second-hand equipment for the novice apiarist.
— Speak to your neighbours about your plans. If you can't put a hive in your garden, talk to local farmers and councils to see if they have any suitable scrubland you can lease for an out apiary.
— Read *Starting with Bees* by Peter Gordon, Broad Leys Publishing, £7.95.

Contacts

— The British Beekeepers' Association, bbka.org.uk: all kinds of bee information, including a list of local associations, guide to events nationwide, a list of holiday cottages and B&Bs owned by beekeepers.
— E.H. Thorne (Beehives) Ltd, thorne.co.uk: hives, clothing, accessories and books. Includes a month-by-month guide to what to do with your hives and details of nationwide beekeeping events.

What's good in March

Vegetables *Broccoli (purple sprouting), Cabbages (various green varieties), Chicory, Greens (spring and winter), Leeks* ***Fruit*** *Rhubarb (forced)* ***Wild greens & herbs*** *Alexanders, Chickweed, Chives, Cow parsley (Wild chervil), Fat hen, Nettles, Sea kale, Watercress* ***Wild flowers & fruits*** *Primroses (garden)* ***Fungi, nuts & saps*** *Birch saps* ***Fish & shellfish*** *Pollack, Salmon (wild), Sea trout, Cockles, Crabs (brown, cock), Oysters (rock)* ***Game*** *Hare*

....

Banana, honey and cinnamon smoothie

Put *3 peeled bananas*, *250g Greek yoghurt*, *50ml whole milk*, *25g porridge oats*, *2 tbsp runny honey*, *1 tsp ground cinnamon*, *1 tsp fresh lemon juice*, *1 tsp peeled and grated fresh ginger* and a *small handful of ice cubes* into a blender and whizz until smooth. Serve in 2 glasses, sprinkled with a little more *cinnamon or a grating of nutmeg*. *Serves 2.*

....

Apricot and honey flapjacks

Preheat the oven to 160°C/Gas Mark 3. Pour boiling water over *140g dried, unsulphured apricots* and leave for 15 minutes to plump up. Melt *250g unsalted butter* in a saucepan over a low heat with *4 tbsp honey*. Mix in *60g light Muscovado sugar* and *60g dark Muscovado sugar* and stir until dissolved. Raise the heat, bring to the boil and let the mixture bubble for a minute or two without stirring until you have a glossy, fudgy mixture. Take the pan off the heat. Combine *250g rolled oats* and *250g jumbo oats* and stir them into the butter mixture. Drain the apricots, pat dry and cut in half. Stir into the oat mixture with the *zest of a lemon and zest of an orange* and *3 tbsp pumpkin seeds*. Mix until everything is very well combined. Butter a 23cm brownie tin and line the bottom with baking parchment. Tip the mixture into the lined tin and smooth the top with a palette knife. Bake for 25–30 minutes, until the edges have darkened and pulled away from the sides slightly and the rest of the flapjack is golden. Remove from the oven, cool for a few minutes, then mark the flapjack into 12 squares with a knife. Leave to cool, then cut along the lines and carefully remove each square from the tin. *Makes 12.*

....

Rhubarb and honey cranachan

Preheat the oven to 200°C/Gas Mark 6. Put *500g rhubarb* cut into 5cm pieces, the *zest of an orange*, *3 tbsp orange juice*, *2 tsp caster sugar* and a *split vanilla pod* into a roasting tin. Stir and bake for 15 minutes or so until soft. Cool the rhubarb completely in its juices, strain off the juices and remove the vanilla pod. Warm a smallish frying pan over a medium-low heat. Add *50g rolled oats* and stir until they are golden and toasted – keep a close eye on them, as they can burn easily. Transfer to a plate to cool. In a medium-sized bowl, stir together *1 tbsp Cointreau* and *284ml double cream* and then whisk until the cream holds soft peaks. Loosely fold in *2 tbsp honey*, the oats and rhubarb, spoon into 4 glasses and serve. *Serves 4.*

Apricot and honey flapjacks

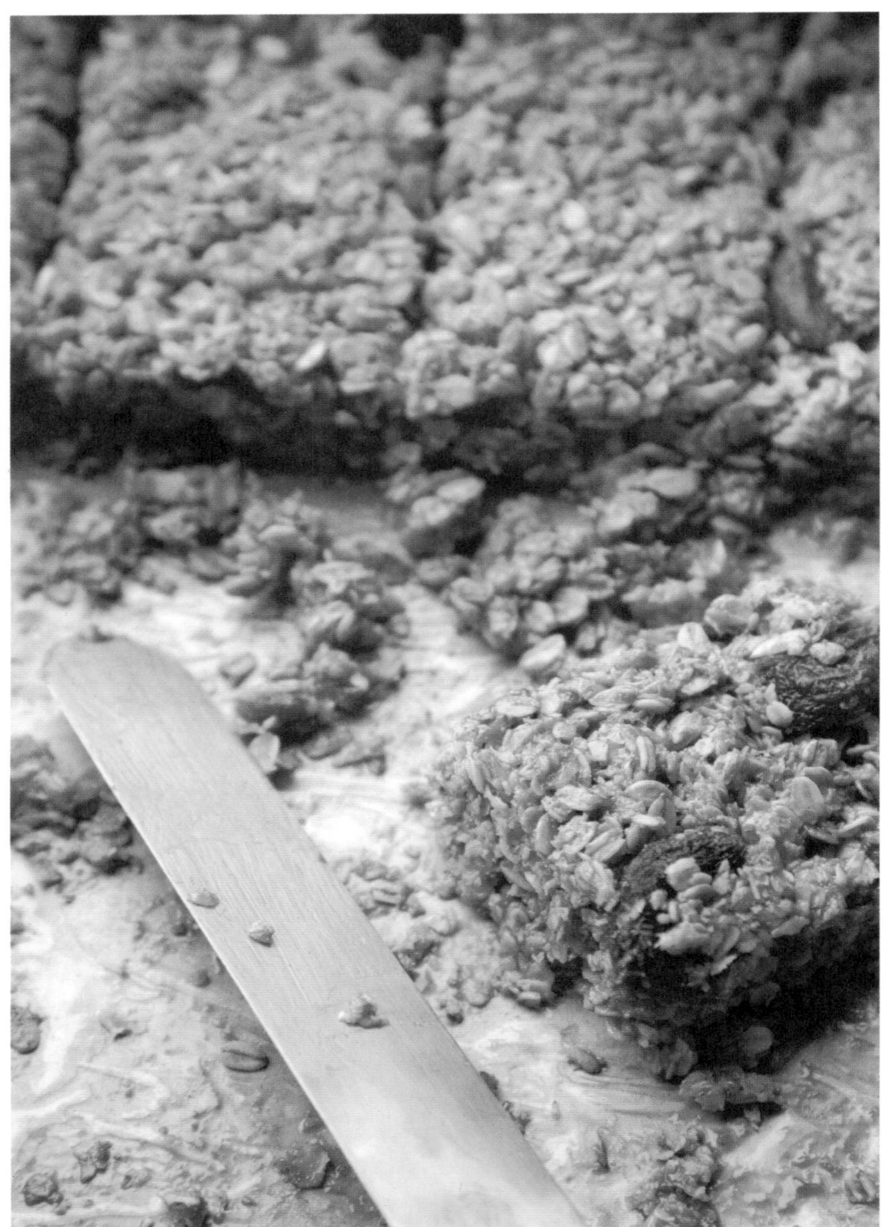

Friday **27**

Saturday **28**

Sunday **1**

St David's Day

Notes

March

2 Monday

3 Tuesday

4 ◐ Wednesday

5 Thursday

Feast East Festival (tasteofanglia.com), until Saturday 7 March

Friday

6

Saturday

7

Sunday

8

Notes

March

9 Monday

10 Tuesday

11 ○ Wednesday

12 Thursday

Friday

13

Saturday

14

Bridport Farmers' Market

Sunday

15

Notes

March

16

Monday

17

Tuesday

St Patrick's Day

18

◑ Wednesday

19

Thursday

Friday

20

Spring Equinox

Saturday

21

Sunday

22

Mothering Sunday

Notes

March

23 Monday

24 Tuesday

25 Wednesday

26 ● Thursday

Friday

27

Saturday

28

Sunday

29

British Summertime begins (clocks forward)

Notes

March

30 Monday

31 Tuesday

1 Wednesday

April Fool's Day

2 ◐ Thursday

April

All about chickens
Pammy Riggs and Richard Hicks

We're thrilled at the explosion of interest in rearing chickens and it doesn't surprise us that our Chicken Day, led by Pammy Riggs and Richard Hicks, is one of our most popular courses. Pammy and Richard are enthusiastic and inspirational experts. They deal cheerfully with all levels of interest, from those who already have their own hens to people who've never even held a chicken before. 'We aim to give people confidence to rear some chickens of their own,' says Pammy, 'to demystify the process.'

Beginning with an introduction to Hugh's birds, Pammy and Richard take a practical approach from the start. The morning's spent fielding all kinds of questions, from how to select the right kind of chicken for your needs, to housing and feeding your happy hens. The afternoon takes visitors from field to kitchen. Everyone gets to eviscerate a bird and prepare it for the table. 'They love it,' says Pammy, 'even the squeamish ones!'

Getting started

— To source your chicks, go to a local farm supply store and look at the notice board, or flip through the advertisements in the back of *Smallholder* magazine; smallholder.co.uk.

— Buy chickens where you can see their environment. If people don't want you to see how they're reared, go elsewhere.

— If you'd like to re-home some battery chickens, contact The Battery Hen Welfare Trust; bhwt.org.uk. They're often pretty robust when given a chance at a normal life.

— Try a Utility Breed, that's a chicken which will provide meat and eggs. Light Sussex or Rhode Island Reds are good varieties for beginners.

— The Henkeepers' Association, henkeepersassociation.co.uk, is a good source of tips, advice and equipment for beginners.

What's good in April

Vegetables *Broccoli (purple sprouting), Cabbages (various green varieties), Cauliflower, Greens (spring and winter), Lettuces, Radish, Sea kale, Sorrel, Watercress* ***Fruit*** *Rhubarb (forced), Rhubarb (outdoor)* ***Wild greens & herbs*** *Alexanders, Chickweed, Chives, Cow parsley (or Wild chervil), Dandelion, Fat hen, Hogweed shoots, Hop shoots, Meadowsweet (leaves), Nettles, Sea spinach, Sorrel, Watercress, Wild garlic, Wild rocket* ***Wild flowers & fruits*** *Primroses (garden)* ***Fungi & nuts*** *Morels, St George's mushrooms* ***Fish & shellfish*** *Cockles, Crabs (brown, cock), Pollack, Salmon (wild), Sea trout* ***Game*** *Wood pigeon*

Hugh's herby roast chicken

Remove the chicken from the fridge an hour before cooking. Preheat the oven to 220°C/Gas Mark 7. Take any string off a *1.5–2kg chicken*, place the bird in a roasting tin, spread its legs out from its body and enlarge the opening of the cavity with your fingers. Put *100g softened butter* into a bowl and throw in *a couple of generous handfuls of roughly chopped thyme, marjoram, chives and parsley* along with a *crushed garlic clove*. Season well with *salt and black pepper* and smear the seasoned butter all over the chicken, inside and out. Put the chicken into the centre of the oven and cook for 25–30 minutes. Baste the chicken, turn the oven down to 180°C/Gas Mark 4, pour *60ml white wine* into the tin and roast for a further 40–60 minutes, depending on its size. To test that the bird is done, pierce the part where the thigh joins the breast; the juices should run clear. Open the oven door, turn off the oven and leave the bird to rest for 15–20 minutes. Carve the bird in the tin, letting all of the pieces fall into the buttery juices. *Serves 4–5.*

Chicken stock

After eating your roast chicken, tear the *carcass* into fairly small pieces and cram them, along with any skin, bones, fat, jelly or burnt bits from the roasting tin, into a saucepan that will take them snugly. If you have the fresh *giblets*, add these too (minus the liver). Add *3–4 roughly chopped celery sticks, 1–2 roughly chopped onions, 1–2 large, roughly chopped carrots, a few chunks of peeled celeriac or parsnip* (optional) and *2 bay leaves, 1 sprig of thyme, a few parsley stalks* and *a few black peppercorns*. Pack everything in as tightly as you can so that you need no more than 1.5 litres of cold water to just cover everything. Bring the pan to a simmer and let it cook, uncovered, for 3–5 hours. Top up the water if necessary. Strain the stock through a fine sieve, leave to cool, then chill immediately. A layer of fat will solidify on the top, which you can scrape off if it's excessive. *Makes 1–1.5 litres.*

Kale and goats' cheese frittata

Preheat the oven to 180°C/Gas Mark 4. Heat *1 tbsp olive oil* and *1 tbsp unsalted butter* in a 25cm non-stick, ovenproof frying pan over a low heat. Add *3 thinly sliced shallots* and cook gently for 10 minutes until soft but not coloured. Remove the tough stems from *180g kale* and chop roughly. Parboil the kale in lightly salted boiling water for 1–2 minutes. Drain well. Whisk *8 free-range eggs* in a medium-sized bowl, season well with *salt, black pepper* and *½ tsp thyme leaves*. Add *200g cooked potatoes* cut into cubes to the shallots, turn over in the fat and warm through slightly. Tip the shallots, potatoes and kale into the bowl with the eggs and pour the whole lot back into the frying pan. Keep the heat low and don't move the ingredients about, just let the eggs solidify slowly from the base up. Break up *125g soft goats' cheese* into chunks, place on top of the frittata and sprinkle with *3 tbsp grated Parmesan*. After about 5 minutes, give the pan a little shake – the bottom half of the frittata should be set but with a good layer of wet egg on top. Place the pan into the oven to finish cooking and remove when just cooked through, about 10 minutes. Cool slightly before slicing and serving. *Serves 4–6.*

Kale and goats' cheese frittata

Friday

3

Saturday

4

Sunday

5

Notes

April

6 Monday

7 Tuesday

8 Wednesday

9 ○ Thursday

Friday **10**

Good Friday (bank holiday)

Saturday **11**

Bridport Farmers' Market

Sunday **12**

Easter Sunday

Notes ***April***

13 Monday

Easter Monday (bank holiday)

14 Tuesday

15 Wednesday

16 Thursday

Friday ◑ **17**

Saturday **18**

Sunday **19**

Notes ***April***

20 Monday

21 Tuesday

22 Wednesday

23 Thursday

St George's Day

Friday

24

Saturday ●

25

Mid Wales Mouthful Food Festival (wonderwoolwales.co.uk/mouthful), until Sunday 26 April

Sunday

26

Notes

April

27 Monday

28 Tuesday

29 Wednesday

30 Thursday

May

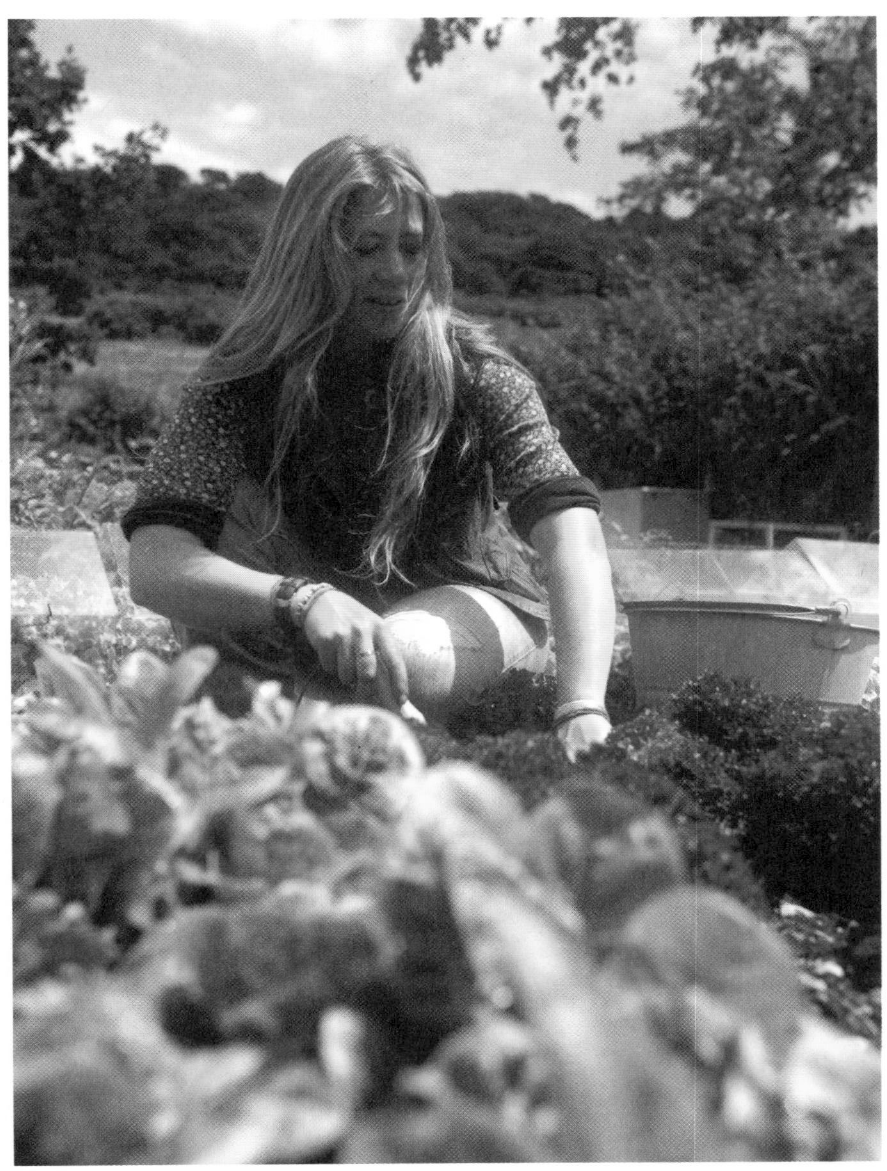

Grab and cook
Emma Stapleforth

At River Cottage, we believe that you're (almost) never too young to wield a trowel and our Grab and Cook days have proved that others feel the same. It's always inspiring to see a group of five- to twelve-year-olds make the unique connection between soil and plate. Emma and the gardening team guide the children through the kitchen garden and the polytunnels, helping them identify herbs, vegetables and fruit, to taste them and select the best specimens for their lunch.

There's nothing like a few hours in the garden for building up an appetite, so we round off the morning with making pizzas outside in the clay oven, slapping together burgers, tossing salads and whizzing up a few fruit smoothies to share in an afternoon picnic with parents.

Getting started

— Grow salads! They taste so much more vibrant when they're fresh and take very little work.

— Start small – gardening should be a pleasure, not a chore. A few pots of parsley, basil, mint, coriander, sage, thyme and rosemary will add savour to so many dishes.

— Grow some edible flowers such as calendula, nasturtiums, borage and roses. They look beautiful in the garden and on the plate.

Contacts

— For a great selection of organic seeds and garden supplies, try Tamar Organics, tamarorganics.co.uk, or Jekka's Herb Farm, jekkasherbfarm.com, for seeds and plants.

What's good in May

Vegetables *Asparagus, Cabbages (various green varieties), Carrots, Cauliflowers, Lettuces, Radishes, Rocket, Sea kale, Sorrel, Watercress* ***Fruit*** *Rhubarb (outdoor)* ***Wild greens & herbs*** *Broom buds, Chives, Dandelions, Fat hen, Hogweed shoots, Hop shoots, Meadowsweet (leaves), Sea spinach, Sorrel, Watercress, Wild fennel, Wild garlic, Wild rocket* ***Fungi & nuts*** *Morels, St George's mushrooms* ***Fish & shellfish*** *Crabs (spider), Signal crayfish (freshwater), Cuttlefish, Pollack, Salmon (wild), Sea trout* ***Game*** *Wood pigeon*

New lettuce with 'soft' hard-boiled egg salad

Wash and gently dry the *leaves from 2–3 lettuces*, ideally a combination of Cos and butterhead types. Keep the leaves mostly whole but perhaps tear the larger ones in half. Put them in a salad bowl. Next, you need *6 'soft' hard-boiled free-range eggs* – the whites should be completely set but the yolks just a bit runny in the middle. To achieve this, put them in a pan of hand-hot water and bring them quickly to the boil, boiling the eggs for exactly 4 minutes (5 if they are extra large). Run them under the cold tap and peel them as soon as they are cool enough to handle. Make a simple vinaigrette by mixing together *4 tbsp olive oil* and *1 tbsp white wine vinegar or cider vinegar*, adding *a pinch of sugar*, *1 tsp Dijon mustard* and *a few grinds of salt and pepper* and shaking it all up in a jar until it's nicely emulsified. Roughly chop the still-warm eggs and put them on top of the lettuce. Chop *6 anchovies* into 1cm pieces and scatter over the eggs. Drizzle the dressing over everything and serve at once. *Serves 4.*

Goats' cheese with yoghurt and herbs

Use a fork to mash together *250g very fresh goats' cheese* and *3–4 tbsp live yoghurt* – you need to add enough yoghurt to get a loose, spoonable, but not quite pourable consistency. Mash a small amount of *garlic*, about a quarter of a clove, with *a pinch of salt* and mix thoroughly into the cheese. Finely chop *a generous bunch of fresh herbs*, majoring on masses of *parsley* and *chives* but including a little *thyme*, *marjoram*, *tarragon* and *chervil*, if you have them. Mix in well, along with *a few grinds of black pepper*. Check and adjust the seasoning, adding more salt, pepper and herbs if necessary. You can serve it at once, but the cheese is best if left to ripen and infuse with flavour for a couple of hours in a cool place or the fridge. Serve with *fresh, crusty bread* and, if you like, *a few Cos lettuce leaves*, *radishes* and *baby carrots* for dipping. *Serves 4–6.*

Warm potato and wilted sorrel salad

Scrub about *500g new potatoes*, such as Jersey Royals, and boil them in well-salted water until just tender. Jersey Royals in particular lose much of their charm if overboiled, so be vigilant and taste a small potato after just 7 minutes or so; 8–10 minutes is often long enough. While the potatoes are cooking, strip the central veins out of *2–3 good handfuls of wild or cultivated sorrel*. Wash well and shred into ribbons about 1cm wide. As soon as the potatoes are ready, drain them and put in a bowl with *about 50g unsalted butter* and *a drizzle of olive oil*. Throw the shredded sorrel into the bowl and toss well. Leave for a minute, so the heat of the potatoes wilts the sorrel, then toss again. Rest for another minute, then season with *a few grinds of fine sea salt and black pepper* and serve at once. *Serves 4 as a starter.*

New lettuce with 'soft' hard-boiled egg salad

Friday ◐ **1**

Saturday **2**

Exeter Festival of South West England Food and Drink (visitsouthwest.co.uk/exeterfoodfestival), until Sunday 3 May

Sunday **3**

Compost Awareness Week (compostawarenessweek.org.uk), until Saturday 9 May

Notes ***May***

4 Monday

May Day (bank holiday)
National Honey Week (honeyassociation.com), until Sunday 10 May
Compost Awareness Week continues until Saturday 9 May

5 Tuesday

6 Wednesday

7 Thursday

Friday **8**

Christchurch Food & Wine Festival (christchurchfoodfest.co.uk), until Sunday 17 May

Saturday ○ **9**

Bridport Farmers' Market

Sunday **10**

Notes ***May***

11 Monday

Christchurch Food & Wine Festival continues until Sunday 17 May

12 Tuesday

13 Wednesday

Balmoral Show (balmoralshow.co.uk), until Friday 15 May

14 Thursday

Royal Windsor Food and Drink Festival (royal-windsor-horse-show.co.uk), until Sunday 17 May

Friday

15

Saturday

16

Derbyshire Food Festival (derbyshirefoodfestival.co.uk), until Sunday 17 May
Henley Food Festival (henleyfoodfestival.co.uk), until Sunday 17 May
Royal Welsh Smallholder and Garden Festival (rwas.co.uk), until Sunday 17 May

Sunday ◑

17

Notes

May

18 Monday

British Tomato Week (britishtomatoes.co.uk), until Sunday 24 May
National Vegetarian Week (vegsoc.org), until Sunday 24 May

19 Tuesday

20 Wednesday

21 Thursday

Devon County Show (devoncountyshow.co.uk), until Saturday 23 May

Friday **22**

Saturday **23**

English Wine Week (englishwineweek.co.uk), until Sunday 31 May
Hertfordshire County Show (hertsshow.com), until Sunday 24 May

Sunday ● **24**

Notes ***May***

25 Monday

Spring Bank Holiday
Surrey County Show (surreycountyshow.co.uk)
Cheese Rolling at Cooper's Hill (cheese-rolling.co.uk)
English Wine Week continues until Sunday 31 May

26 Tuesday

27 Wednesday

Suffolk Show (suffolkshow.co.uk), until Thursday 28 May
Royal Bath and West Show (bathandwest.com), until Saturday 30 May

28 Thursday

Friday 29

Saturday 30

Sunday ◐ 31

Notes ***May***

1 Monday

2 Tuesday

3 Wednesday

4 Thursday

Royal Cornwall Show (royalcornwallshow.org), until Saturday 6 June

June

Edible seashore
John Wright

Edible Seashore days with our foraging expert, John Wright, are a briny treasure hunt, following the tides and searching out the best locations for a host of different food species. Visitors begin the day at the beach where there will no doubt be some sea beet, sea campion, and – John's personal favourite – sea kale, a rare and magnificent plant that springs up, triffid-like, from the shingle. There's often sea blite, samphire, rock samphire and wild rocket, so strong that when you taste it, says John, 'You know why it's called rocket – it'll take your head off!'

And then it's out to the mud flats on the other side of Portland with Troy, a scallop fisherman who helps in the hunt for cockles and carpet clams. The highlight for many is watching Troy tip salt down the razor clams' keyholes in the sand and seeing them pop up from their damp hiding place. Next, visitors collect some edible seaweeds such as carrageen, dulse, kelp and laver. And the reward for gathering this bounty? To round off the day, the River Cottage chefs use it as part of a seaside banquet back at the farm.

Getting started

— Start by familiarising yourself with a few seaweeds; carrageen, dulse, kelp and laver are all safe to eat.
— Get to know your local coastline – there's always something to discover. You'd be very unlucky to come home without some sea beet and rock samphire.
— When gathering, collect just a little from each plant and make sure you cut things – don't uproot them without permission from the landowner.

Contacts

— If you're hunting for shellfish, make sure they're from a clean environment. Your local Environmental Agency office can tell you if the beach is safe; environment-agency.gov.uk, or use the Marine Conservation Society's website; goodbeachguide.co.uk.

What's good in June

Vegetables *Asparagus, Broad beans, Carrots, Cauliflowers, Lettuces, Peas (including sugar snap), Purslane, Radishes, Rocket, Sorrel, Watercress* ***Fruit*** *Cherries (European), Gooseberries, Rhubarb (outdoor), Strawberries* ***Wild greens & herbs*** *Broom buds, Horseradish, Marsh samphire, Sea spinach, Wild fennel* ***Wild flowers & fruits*** *Elderflowers* ***Fungi & nuts*** *Horse mushrooms, Fairy ring champignons* ***Fish & shellfish*** *Black bream, Crabs (spider), Signal crayfish (fresh-water), Cuttlefish, Mackerel, Pollack, Salmon (wild), Sea bass, River trout (brown and rainbow), Sea trout* ***Game*** *Wood pigeon*

Samphire with poached eggs

Bring two pans of water to the boil. Carefully pick over about *350g samphire*, removing roots and tough stems. Rinse thoroughly to get rid of any grit, then break up any larger, multi-branched pieces into smaller pieces. Toss the samphire into one of the pans of boiling water – do not add salt as the samphire is already very salty – and boil for a couple of minutes. Drain well and toss with *a knob of butter* and some *black pepper* and return to the pan to keep warm. Crack *2 free-range eggs* into a saucer. Make sure the second pan of water is boiling vigorously, add *1 tbsp cider vinegar* and stir the water with a wooden spoon to create a whirlpool. Tip the eggs into the whirlpool. Turn the heat down low and poach for about 3 minutes until the whites are set. Remove eggs with a slotted spoon and drain on kitchen paper. Divide the samphire between two warmed plates, place a poached egg on top of each one and grind on some black pepper. Serve immediately. *Serves 2.*

Potted shrimp

Gently melt *120g unsalted butter* in a small saucepan. Pour it into another saucepan, leaving behind any of the milky solids. Reserve 2–3 tbsp of the clarified butter in a small, warmed jug. To the rest of the clarified butter, add *a pinch of mace*, *a pinch of cayenne pepper* and *a bay leaf*. Simmer very gently for 2 minutes. Remove the bay leaf, add *200g cooked and peeled brown shrimps or rockpool prawns* and *a squeeze of lemon juice*. Stir for a couple of minutes, season with *a little salt and freshly ground white pepper*, and remove from the heat. Spoon into two ramekins, cover with a thin layer of the reserved clarified butter and put into the fridge to set. Remove from the fridge 20 minutes or so before you want to serve them, spread over hot brown toast. *Serves 2.*

Smoked pollack with sea beet

Put *two fillets of smoked pollack* (see November to make your own) into a medium-sized saucepan and pour over *150ml whole milk* and *150ml double cream*. Cover the pan and bring to a gentle simmer. Turn off the heat and let the fish cook in the hot liquid – this may only take another minute. Lift out the pollack and keep warm. Turn up the heat and reduce the liquid to half its volume. Wash *2 big handfuls of sea beet* and shred into 3–4cm pieces. Warm *a knob of butter* in a frying pan and sauté the sea beet until it's just wilted and still bright green. Add half of the milk and cream mixture to the frying pan and cook until the liquid thickens and the sea beet is well coated. Add *a squirt of lemon juice* and *some black pepper* (it may not need salt as the fish is quite salty). Divide the sea beet between two warm plates, top with the smoked pollack and serve immediately with *lemon wedges* and slices of *brown bread and butter*. *Serves 2.*

Potted shrimp

Friday **5**

Royal Cornwall Show continues until Saturday 6 June

Saturday **6**

Sunday ○ **7**

Open Farm Sunday (farmsunday.org)

Notes ***June***

8 Monday

9 Tuesday

10 Wednesday

11 Thursday

South of England Show (seas.org.uk), until Saturday 13 June

Friday **12**

Saturday **13**

Bridport Farmers' Market

Sunday **14**

Notes ***June***

15 ◑ Monday

16 Tuesday

17 Wednesday

18 Thursday

Friday **19**

East of England Show (eastofengland.org.uk), until Sunday 21 June

Saturday **20**

World Stinging Nettle Eating Championships and Beer Festival (thebottleinn.co.uk)

Sunday **21**

Summer Solstice (nmm.ac.uk)
Father's Day

Notes ***June***

22 ● Monday

23 Tuesday

Cheshire County Show (cheshirecountyshow.org.uk), until Wednesday 24 June

24 Wednesday

25 Thursday

Royal Highland Show (royalhighlandshow.org), until Sunday 28 June

Friday **26**

Glastonbury Festival (glastonburyfestivals.co.uk), until Sunday 28 June

Saturday **27**

Colchester Food and Drink Festival (colchesterfoodanddrinkfestival.co.uk), until Sunday 28 June
Pembrokeshire Fish Week (fishweek.co.uk), until Sunday 5 July

Sunday **28**

Notes ***June***

29 ◐ Monday

Pembrokeshire Fish Week continues until Sunday 5 July

30 Tuesday

1 Wednesday

Hampshire Food Festival (hampshirefare.co.uk), until Friday 31 July
Royal Norfolk Show (royalnorfolkshow.co.uk), until Thursday 2 July

2 Thursday

July

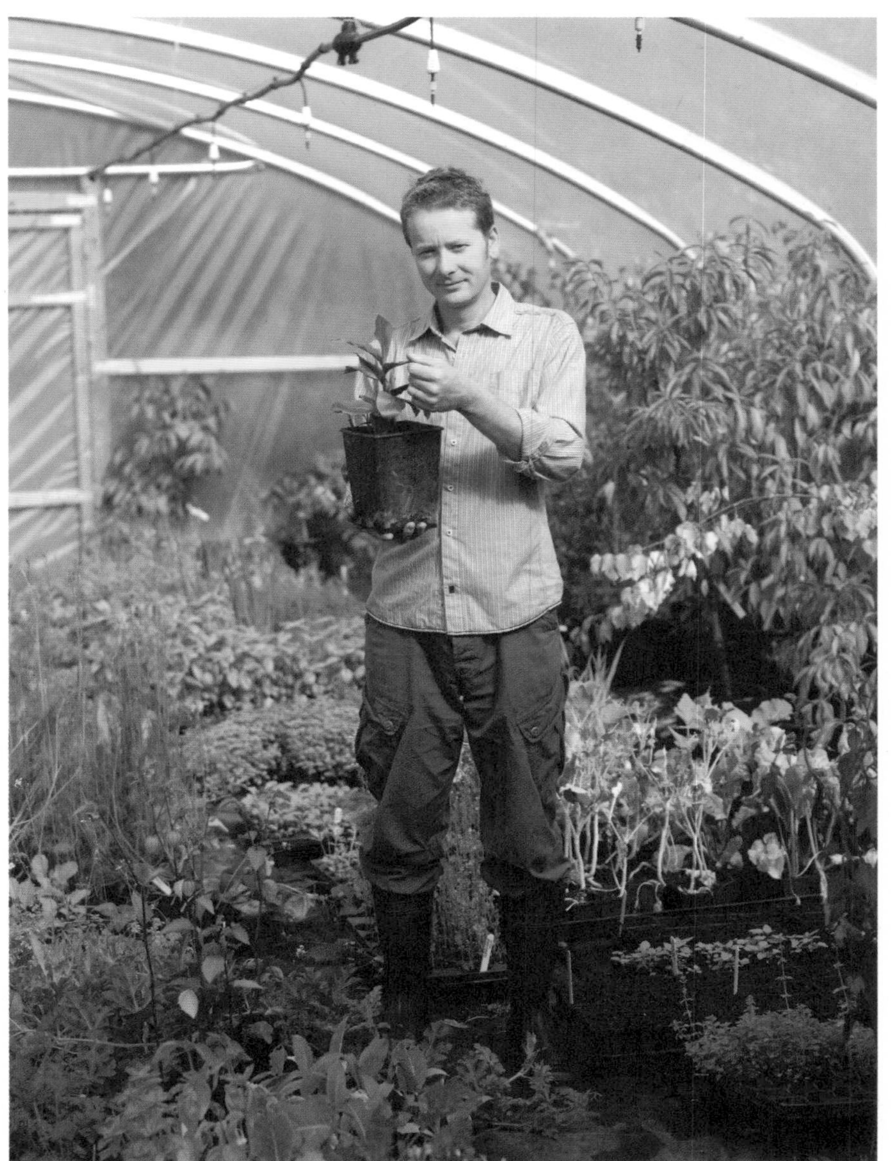

Climate-change garden
Mark Diacono

This month, we're looking to the future with Mark Diacono, our climate-change gardening expert. On his own seventeen acres at Otter Farm, just outside Honiton, he's cultivating an edible forest of bounty not usually grown here, such as peaches, nectarines, almonds and olives, along with spices such as Szechuan, Japanese sancho and Nepalese pepper. And here at Park Farm he's begun to do the same for us, creating our own climate-change garden which will be the focus of an exciting new course.

As more and more of us become aware of the universal challenges that face us, Mark generates optimism about growing and gardening in a whole new way. 'It makes sense,' he says. 'Taking advantage of the changing climate to grow the things we normally have to import doesn't just save on food miles, it has a massive impact on flavour. Peaches picked before they're perfectly ripe may soften in transit but they certainly won't get any sweeter.'

Getting started

— Grow things you love to eat. This makes all of the effort you put in so much more rewarding.

— If you have limited space, grow things that aren't readily available. How much more exciting to have your own Szechuan pepper than a plot full of nothing but spuds!

— Take time to research new varieties of plants, shrubs and trees that are less susceptible to pests and diseases and often produce earlier.

Contacts

— Get in touch with the Agroforestry Research Trust, agroforestry.co.uk, for information, books, and fruit and nut trees and bushes by mail order.

— Check out Mark's own website, otterfarm.co.uk, to order plants and find out more about climate-change gardening throughout the year.

What's good in July

Vegetables *Artichokes (globe), Beetroot, Broad beans, Carrots, Cauliflowers, Courgettes, French beans (whole pod), Garlic, Kohlrabi, Lamb's lettuce, Onions, Pak choi, Peas (including sugar snaps), Potatoes, Purslane, Radishes, Rocket, Sorrel, Spinach, Tomatoes, Watercress* ***Fruit*** *Apricots, Blackcurrants, Blueberries, Cherries (European and home-grown), Gooseberries, Raspberries, Redcurrants, Rhubarb (outdoor), Strawberries, White currants, Worcesterberries* ***Wild greens & herbs*** *Horseradish, Marsh samphire, Wild fennel* ***Wild flowers & fruits*** *Elderflowers, Wild strawberries* ***Fungi & nuts*** *Chanterelles, Chicken of the woods, Summer truffles* ***Fish & shellfish*** *Black bream, Crabs (brown, hen and spider), Signal crayfish (freshwater), Lobsters, Mackerel, Pollack, Scallops, Sea bass, Sea trout, River trout (brown and rainbow)* ***Game*** *Rabbit, Wood pigeon*

Salt and pepper squid

Toast *2 tsp Szechuan peppercorns* and *1 tsp black peppercorns* in a small, non-stick pan for a couple of minutes until they become fragrant. Remove from the heat and tip into a pestle and mortar or a spice grinder with *½ tsp chilli flakes* and *2 tbsp sea salt* and grind until well combined. Whisk the salt and pepper mixture with *120g cornflour* until well combined. Heat about *750ml–1 litre groundnut or sunflower oil* in a deep-fat fryer or a heavy pan to a temperature of 180°C. (If you don't have a cooking thermometer, test that it's hot enough by dropping a small piece of bread into the oil – it should turn golden brown in one minute.) Cut about *500g cleaned squid* into 1cm rings – keep the tentacles whole – and toss a few pieces of squid in the seasoned flour. The easiest way to do this is to place the squid in a sieve with a few tablespoons of the flour. Shake the sieve until the flour has evenly coated the squid and any excess has dropped through. Put the squid in the hot oil a few pieces at a time and fry for 1–1½ minutes until golden. Transfer to a tray lined with kitchen paper and continue to cook the rest. Serve straight away with *lemon wedges*. *Serves 4 as a starter.*

Spiced almonds

Heat a *3–4 tbsp olive oil* in a large frying pan over a medium heat and gently sauté *2 big handfuls of whole, blanched almonds*, stirring constantly, until lightly golden, about 5 minutes. Drain on kitchen paper. In a medium-sized bowl, combine *1 tbsp fresh thyme leaves*, *1 tsp ground cumin*, *½ tsp flaky sea salt*, *a large pinch of smoked paprika* and *a large pinch of cayenne*. Toss the almonds in the spice mixture until they are well coated. Serve warm or cold. These will keep for a couple of weeks in an airtight jar.

Apricots on toast

Preheat the oven to 190°C/Gas Mark 5. Halve about *16 apricots* and remove their stones. Arrange them in a baking dish, cut side up. Snip *2 vanilla pods* into pieces about 1cm long. Put a piece of vanilla in the hollow at the centre of each apricot, along with *a tiny scrap of butter* and *a sprinkling of caster sugar*. Roast the apricots for around 15 minutes, or until they are tender when pierced with a knife and their syrupy juices are running. Toast *4 thick slices of crusty white bread or brioche loaf* and spread generously with more *butter*. Spoon the apricots and their hot, sticky juices on to the toast and serve straight away, with *dollops of clotted cream or ice cream* if you'd like to make more of an event of it. *Serves 4.*

Apricots on toast

Friday

3

Pembrokeshire Fish Week continues until Sunday 5 July
Hampshire Food Festival continues until Friday 31 July

Saturday

4

Sunday

5

Notes

July

6 Monday

Hampshire Food Festival continues until Friday 31 July

7 ○ Tuesday

8 Wednesday

9 Thursday

Royal Show (royalshow.org.uk), until Sunday 12 July

Friday

10

Saturday

11

Bridport Farmers' Market

Sunday

12

Notes

July

13 Monday

Hampshire Food Festival continues until Friday 31 July

14 Tuesday

Great Yorkshire Show (greatyorkshireshow.org.uk), until Thursday 16 July

15 ◑ Wednesday

16 Thursday

Friday

17

Kent Show (kentshowground.co.uk), until Sunday 19 July

Saturday

18

Cumberland Show (cumberlandshow.co.uk)

Sunday

19

Notes

July

20 Monday

Royal Welsh Show (rwas.co.uk), until Thursday 23 July
Hampshire Food Festival continues until Friday 31 July

21 Tuesday

22 ● Wednesday

23 Thursday

Friday **24**

Border Union Show (buas.org), until Saturday 25 July
CLA Game Fair (gamefair.co.uk), until Sunday 26 July

Saturday **25**

Tavistock Food and Drink Festival (tavistockfoodfestival.co.uk), until Sunday 26 July

Sunday **26**

Notes ***July***

27 Monday

Hampshire Food Festival continues until Friday 31 July

28 ◐ Tuesday

Nantwich International Cheese Show (nantwichshow.co.uk), until Wednesday 29 July
New Forest and Hampshire Show (newforestshow.co.uk), until Thursday 30 July

29 Wednesday

30 Thursday

August

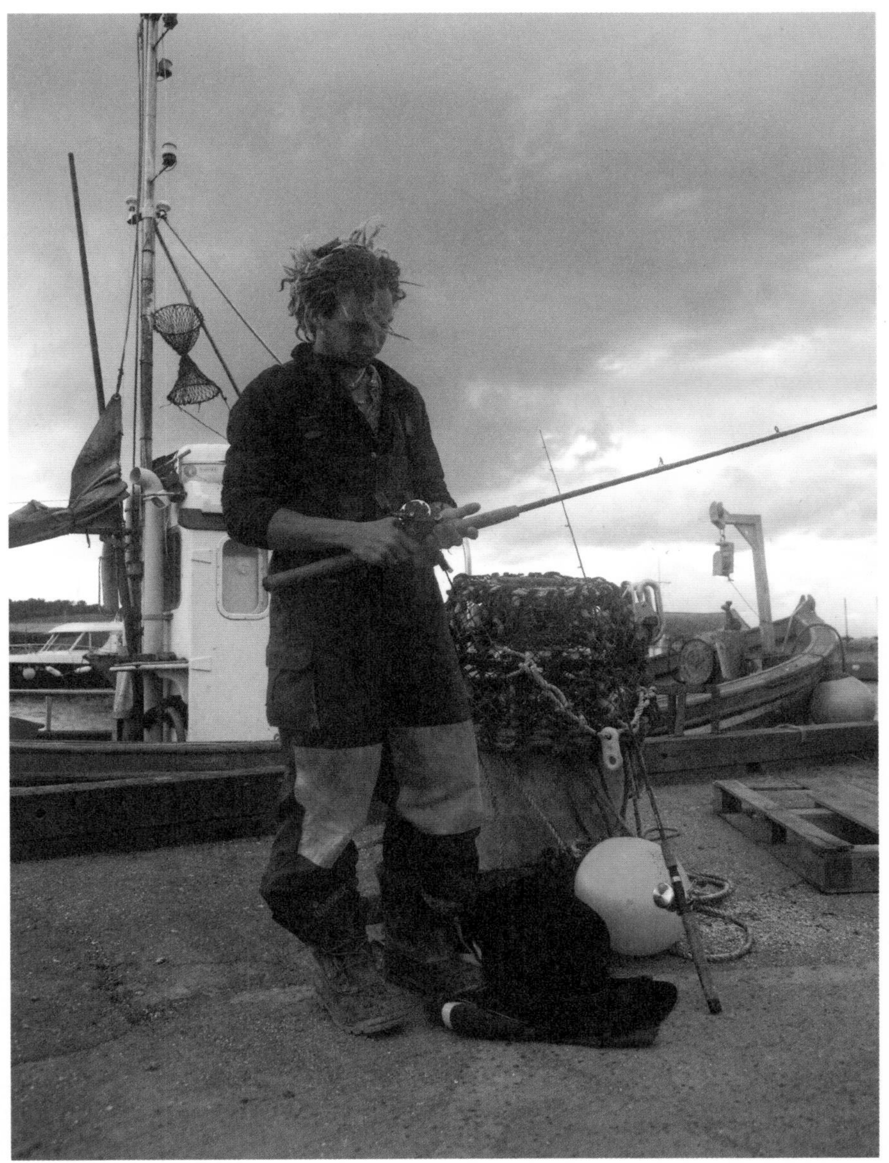

Catch and cook
Tom Lichfield

On Catch and Cook days, it's a case of the early bird catches the fish. Visitors assemble on The Cobb at Lyme Regis at 8 a.m. before heading off with boat host Tom Lichfield. Tom says, 'Many people are happy to catch the fish but are nervous about taking them off the hook, or even touching them. It comes as a surprise to handle fish this fresh when you're used to seeing them all prepped up on the fishmonger's slab.'

At lunchtime, visitors head back to Park Farm where the chefs demonstrate the many delicious dishes we can make with the haul – at this time of year, it can include black bream, bass, whiting and mackerel. While it's cooking, Tom and his team show visitors how to gut and fillet. Tom says, 'It's great to see people who were timid at the beginning of the day wielding the knife as they gut and fillet. It's all about building confidence.' And the reward? A fishy feast in the barn.

Getting started

— When buying fish, eyes should be clear and vibrant, gills should be red and the fish firm to the touch. The fish should smell fresh, clean and 'of the sea' but not 'fishy'.

— Don't buy fish with a recipe in mind. Buy the freshest you can and make the recipe around that.

— If you'd like to start fishing, go to your local tackle shop and talk to the people there. Fishing is a social sport and keen fishermen usually can't wait to share their knowledge.

Contacts

— The National Federation of Sea Anglers: nfsa.org.uk.

— The Marine Conservation Society's website fishonline.org offers advice on catching fish with minimal damage to marine wildlife and habitats.

What's good in August

Vegetables *Globe artichokes, Aubergines, Beetroots, Broad beans, Broccoli (Calabrese), Cabbages (various green varieties), Carrots, Cauliflowers, Chard, Courgettes, Cucumbers, Fennel, French beans (whole pod), Garlic, Kohlrabi, Lamb's lettuce, Lettuces, Onions, Pak choi, Peas (including sugar snaps), Potatoes, Purslane, Radishes, Rocket, Runner beans, Salsify (and Scorzonera), Samphire, Sorrel, Spinach, Sweetcorn, Tomatoes, Watercress* ***Fruit*** *Apples, early (Discovery, George Cave, Redsleeves), Apricots, Blackberries (cultivated), Blackcurrants, Blueberries, Loganberries, Plums, Raspberries, Redcurrants, White currants, Worcesterberries* ***Wild greens & herbs*** *Horseradish, Marsh samphire, Wild fennel* ***Wild flowers & fruits*** *Bilberries (Blaeberries), Blackberries, Bullace, Wild strawberries* ***Fungi & nuts*** *Ceps (Porcini), Chanterelles, Chicken of the woods, Field mushrooms, Giant puffballs, Hazelnuts, Horse mushrooms, Oyster mushrooms (Pleurottes), Parasols, Summer truffles* ***Fish & shellfish*** *Black bream, Crabs (brown, hen and spider), Signal crayfish (freshwater), Lobsters, Mackerel, Pollack, Prawns, Scallops, Sea bass, Squid, River trout (brown and rainbow)* ***Game*** *Rabbit, Wood pigeon*

Devilled crab

Preheat the oven to 190°C/Gas Mark 5. Put a large, heavy-bottomed pan over a medium heat and add *50g unsalted butter*. Toss in *1 large, finely chopped onion* and sweat gently for 10 minutes. Pour in *100ml sherry* and let it boil for a few seconds. Add *2 tbsp cider vinegar*, *1½ tbsp Worcestershire sauce* and bring to the boil. Stir in *1 rounded tsp English mustard*, *1 tsp cayenne pepper* and *200ml double cream*. Simmer for 2 minutes until it thickens slightly. Remove from the heat and fold the *cooked brown and white meat from 2 brown, spider or velvet swimmer crabs* (clean the shells and reserve). Season well with *salt*, *black pepper* and *a little lemon juice*. Spoon the mixture back into the crab shells or into individual gratin dishes. Sprinkle with *50g fresh white breadcrumbs* and dot with *a little butter*. Place on a baking tray and bake for 20–25 minutes until bubbling and golden. Serve hot with *thickly buttered toast* and *a green salad*. *Serves 2.*

Mackerel and puy lentil salad

Preheat the oven to 200°C/Gas Mark 6. Rub *2–3 whole gutted mackerel* with *a little olive oil*, season well with *salt and black pepper*, put in a roasting tin and bake, uncovered, for 12–15 minutes. Alternatively, barbecue them for 3–4 minutes per side. Set aside and cool. Rinse 200g Puy lentils and put them in a large saucepan with *1 celery stick*, cut into 3 pieces, *2 carrots* cut into 3 pieces, *2 bashed but unpeeled garlic cloves*, *½ onion* and *a few parsley stalks*. Cover with cold water, bring to a gentle simmer and skim off any scum that rises to the surface. Simmer until the lentils are al dente, about 20 minutes. Strain the lentils, discarding the water and vegetables. Pick all of the flesh from the mackerel and flake it, discarding any bones, and place it in a bowl with the warm lentils. Add *1 small finely sliced red onion*, *4 finely chopped anchovy fillets*, *1 tbsp rinsed and chopped baby capers* and *2 tbsp chopped parsley*. Stir in *a glug of extra virgin olive oil*, then season to taste with *lemon juice*, *salt and black pepper*. Toss gently and serve straight away. *Serves 4.*

Pollack brandade

Scatter *50g coarse sea salt* on to the base of a large non-metallic dish. Lay *500g pollack*, ling or whiting fillets, skin side down, on the salt. Scatter a further *50g coarse sea salt* evenly over the top and refrigerate for 15 minutes. Then gently but quickly rinse off the salt under the cold tap. Bring a pan of water to a simmer, add the lightly salted fillets and poach for 3–5 minutes, until just cooked. Set aside to cool a little, then flake the fish off its skin, removing any bones. Boil *1kg peeled potatoes* in lightly salted water until tender and drain well. Crush the potatoes lightly with a potato masher or wooden spoon, to form a rough, chunky mash. Heat *a good knob of butter* and *1–2 tbsp olive oil* in a small frying pan and gently sweat *2 finely chopped garlic cloves* for a couple of minutes, without browning. Take off the heat, and stir in *2 tbsp finely chopped parsley and/or chives*. Combine the flaked fish, rough mash, garlicky, herby butter and oil. Season well with *black pepper* and serve, just warm, with *a crisp lettuce salad* on the side. *Serves 4.*

Devilled crab

Friday **31**

Last day of Hampshire Food Festival

Saturday **1**

Sunday **2**

Notes **August**

3 Monday

Bank Holiday (Scotland)

4 Tuesday

Great British Beer Festival (gbbf.org), until Saturday 8 August

5 Wednesday

6 ○ Thursday

Friday **7**

Saturday **8**

Bridport Farmers' Market

Sunday **9**

Notes ***August***

10 Monday

11 Tuesday

12 Wednesday

13 ◑ Thursday

Friday **14**

Saturday **15**

Sunday **16**

Notes ***August***

17 Monday

18 Tuesday

19 Wednesday

20 ● Thursday

Friday **21**

Saturday **22**

Isle of Wight Garlic Festival (garlic-festival.co.uk), until Sunday 23 August

Sunday **23**

Notes ***August***

24 Monday

25 Tuesday

26 Wednesday

27 ◐ Thursday

Melplash Show (melplashshow.co.uk)

Friday

28

Saturday

29

Sunday

30

Notes

August

31 Monday

Summer Bank Holiday

1 Tuesday

Brighton and Hove Food and Drink Festival (brightonfoodfestival.co.uk), until Wednesday 30 September

2 Wednesday

3 Thursday

Bucks County Show (buckscountyshow.co.uk)

September

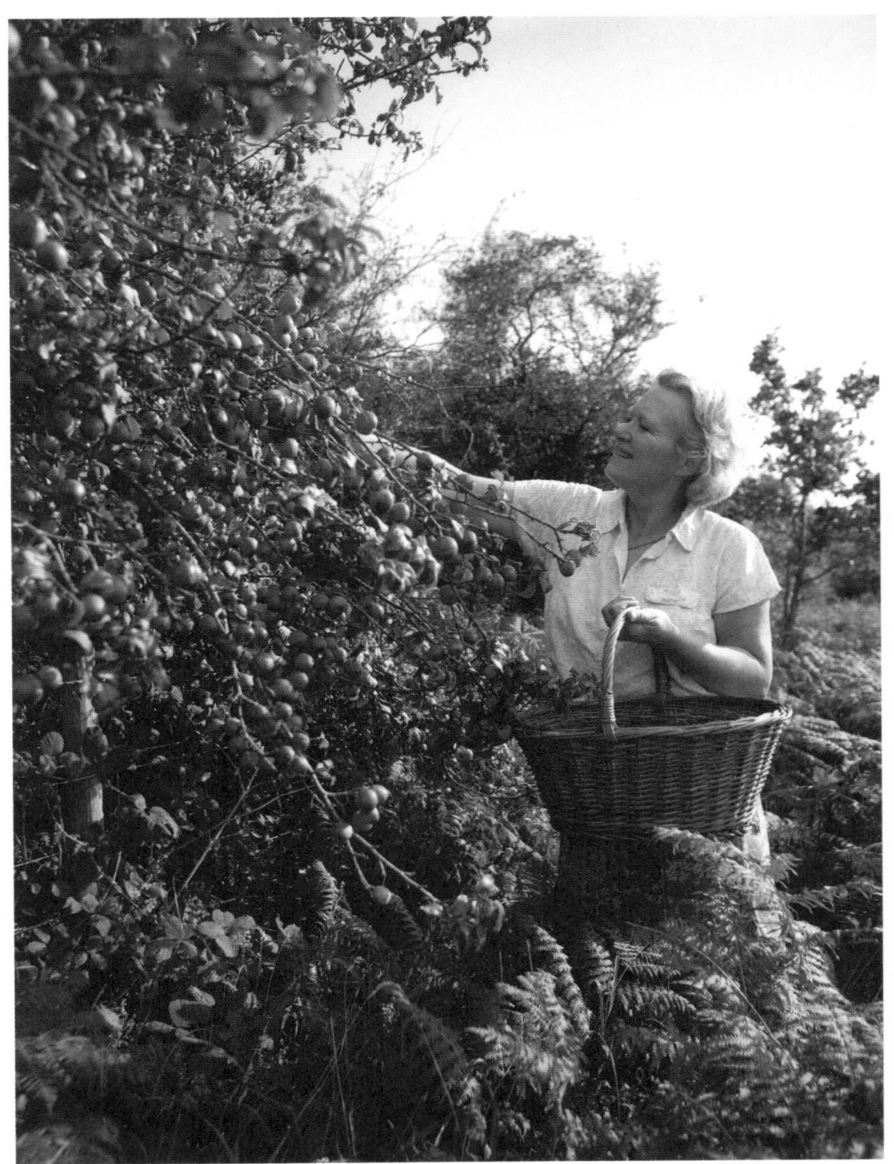

Garden glut
Pam Corbin

Preserving days at Park Farm are steamy, sweet and spicy and right in the middle of all the activity is Pam Corbin, known affectionately around here as 'Pam the Jam' because of her passion for – and unsurpassed knowledge of – all things jarred, preserved and bottled.

At this time of year, when the fruit and veg patch, orchard and hedgerows are bursting with life, Pam doesn't waste a minute, or a morsel of produce. 'The delight is that home grown or hedgerow grown, you know what's in the jar,' she explains.

The first thing visitors to Pam's class see is the barn crammed with baskets overflowing with what seems like half of the garden. During the day, they watch the contents of these baskets being transformed into jams, jellies, curds and fruit cheeses, chutneys and cordials. 'There is nothing more satisfying than seeing all of the jars laid out on the table,' says Pam. 'It's simple and hugely rewarding.'

Getting started

- Good food hygiene is essential. Make sure everything is scrupulously clean before you start.
- Always use fresh, dry, slightly under-ripe fruit for jam.
- When making chutney, take care to chop all of the fruit and vegetables to the same size. It may be time consuming, but it makes all the difference to the finished texture.
- To learn more about preserving, check out *River Cottage Handbook No.2: Preserves* by Pam Corbin, Bloomsbury, £12.99.

Contacts

- For preserving pans, jars, labels and other equipment, try waresofknutsford.co.uk or lakeland.co.uk.
- For organic and fair trade spices and spice infusions, contact steenbergsorganic.net.

What's good in September

Vegetables *Globe artichokes, Aubergines, Beetroot, Borlotti beans (for podding), Broccoli (Calabrese), Cabbages (various green varieties), Carrots, Cauliflowers, Chard, Courgettes, Cucumbers, Fennel, Garlic, Kale (and Borecole), Kohlrabi, Lamb's lettuce, Onions, Pak choi, Peppers and chillies, Pumpkins (and Squash), Rocket, Runner beans, Salsify (and Scorzonera), Sorrel, Spinach, Sweetcorn, Tomatoes, Watercress* ***Fruit*** *Apple, early (Discovery, George Cave, Redsleeves), Apple, late (Egremont Russet, Blenheim Orange, Orleans Reinette), Blackberries, Blueberries, Damsons, Greengages, Loganberries, Pears, early-mid (Beth, William, Merton Pride), Plums* ***Wild greens & herbs*** *Horseradish* ***Wild flowers & fruits*** *Bilberries (Blaeberries), Blackberries, Bullace, Elderberries, Juniper berries* ***Fungi & nuts*** *Ceps (Porcini), Chanterelles, Chicken of the woods, Field mushrooms, Giant puffballs, Hazelnuts, Horse mushrooms, Oyster mushrooms (Pleurottes), Parasols, Shaggy ink caps, Summer truffles* ***Fish & shellfish*** *Black bream, Crabs (brown, hen and spider), Signal crayfish (freshwater), Eels, Lobsters, Mackerel, Mussels, Oysters, Prawns, Scallops, Sea bass, Sprats, Squid, River trout (brown and rainbow), Salmon (wild)* ***Game*** *Goose (farmed), Grey squirrel, Grouse, Mallard, Rabbit, Wood pigeon*

Hugh's raspberry fridge jam

Pick over *1.5kg raspberries*, discarding any leaves, stalks or fruit which is less than perfect. Put half of the fruit in a preserving pan or a wide, deep, heavy-based saucepan which allows enough room to let the jam bubble away safely. Use a potato masher to lightly crush the fruit. Add the rest of the raspberries and *750g jam sugar* with added pectin. Stir over a low heat to dissolve the sugar, then bring quickly to a rolling boil and boil for exactly 5 minutes (for a firmer, more set jam, boil for a further 2–3 minutes). Remove from the heat and stir to disperse any scum. Cool for 5 minutes to prevent the pips rushing to the top of the jar. Pot up in jam jars that have been sterilised by being washed in hot, soapy water and dried in a low oven (or jars still hot from being put through a dishwasher cycle). Cover with a wax disc while hot, then with a cellophane cover or a screw-top lid. Once opened, refrigerate the jam and use within two or three weeks. *Makes 6 x 340g jars.*

Honeyed hazelnuts

Crack *500g hazelnuts or cobnuts* and remove the kernels. Heat a frying pan over a low heat. Add the shelled nuts in batches and toast for 4–5 minutes – shake the pan frequently to make sure they don't burn. Remove from the heat and allow to cool. Pack the nuts into a sterilised jar (see Hugh's raspberry fridge jam for method), adding *1 tbsp clear honey* every third or fourth layer. Continue until the jar is full, making sure the nuts are well covered with honey – you will use up to 340g. Seal securely with a lid and store in a cool, dry place. Use within 12 months – over Greek yoghurt, ice cream or porridge. *Makes 2 x 225g jars.*

Sweet cucumber pickle

Using the slicing blade of a food processor or a very sharp knife, very finely slice *1kg cucumbers*. Peel *3 small red or white onions* and slice them very thinly too. Combine with the cucumber and *1 tbsp chopped dill* in a large bowl. In a separate bowl, mix *250g granulated sugar*, *1 tbsp salt* and *200ml cider vinegar* and pour over the cucumbers and onions. Leave overnight for the sweet and sour flavours to mingle. Pack into a large, airtight container and store in the fridge for up to two weeks. The pickle is delicious in all kinds of salads and sandwiches or with hot-smoked fish. Makes *2 x 450g jars.*

Sweet cucumber pickle

Friday ○ **4**

Brighton and Hove Food and Drink Festival continues until Wednesday 30 September

Saturday **5**

Dorset Show (dorsetcountyshow.co.uk), until Sunday 6 September

Sunday **6**

Notes

September

7 Monday

Brighton and Hove Food and Drink Festival continues until Wednesday 30 September

8 Tuesday

9 Wednesday

10 Thursday

Friday **11**

Ludlow Food Festival (foodfestival.co.uk), until Sunday 13 September

Saturday ◑ **12**

Bridport Farmers' Market
Sturminster Newton Cheese Festival (cheesefestival.co.uk), until Sunday 13 September

Sunday **13**

Notes ***September***

14 Monday

Brighton and Hove Food and Drink Festival continues until Wednesday 30 September

15 Tuesday

16 Wednesday

17 Thursday

Friday ● **18**

York Festival of Food & Drink (yorkfoodfestival.com), until Sunday 27 September
Abergavenny Food Festival (abergavennyfoodfestival.com), until Saturday 19 September

Saturday **19**

British Food Fortnight (britishfoodfortnight.co.uk), until Sunday 4 October

Sunday **20**

Notes ***September***

21 Monday

York Festival of Food & Drink continues until Sunday 27 September
Brighton and Hove Food and Drink Festival continues until Wednesday 30 September
British Food Fortnight continues until Sunday 4 October

22 Tuesday

Autumn Equinox

23 Wednesday

24 Thursday

Friday **25**

Saturday ◐ **26**

Great British Cheese Festival (thecheeseweb.com), until Sunday 27 September

Sunday **27**

Notes ***September***

28 Monday

Brighton and Hove Food and Drink Festival continues until Wednesday 30 September
British Food Fortnight continues until Sunday 4 October

29 Tuesday

30 Wednesday

1 Thursday

October

Foraging
Steven Lamb

At River Cottage, we're wild about wild food, and few more so than Steven Lamb who assists John Wright (see June) on our Walk on the Wildside Mushroom Foraging days.

The adventure starts early, at 7 a.m. with a foragers' breakfast of homemade sausages, bacon and eggs, before we head out for the hunt. In the course of the morning, Steve and John share some of the secrets of finding the best haul and how to spot the conditions in grassland and woodland which might bring a twinkle to any mycologist's eye.

Of course, with mushrooms it's not just about food. It's as important to seek out the poisonous ones – and learn to identify them – as the edible ones. There are over 4,000 varieties of mushroom in the UK and only about a hundred or so are fit to eat. Steve and John aim to take the fear out of fungus and, with luck, collectors will return to the farm with baskets heavy with ceps, wood blewits and chanterelles. John's lively talks are always a great favourite, and discussions of the mysterious charms of fungi continue over a special mushroom feast prepared by our chefs.

Getting started

— The best introduction is to join in a guided walk with an experienced mycologist.

— Swat up with the *River Cottage Handbook No.1: Mushrooms* by John Wright, Bloomsbury, £12.99. Start by familiarising yourself with five edible and five poisonous mushrooms.

— Check out fungus.org.uk or The Association of British Fungus Groups, abfg.org, for information on regional groups, talks and mushroom walks.

— Never, ever eat anything you're not sure about.

What's good in October

Vegetables *Beetroots, Borlotti beans (for podding), Broccoli (Calabrese), Cabbages (various green varieties), Cardoons, Carrots, Cauliflowers, Celeriac, Celery, Chard, Courgettes, Fennel, Kale (and Borecole), Kohlrabi, Leeks, Onions, Peppers and chillies, Potatoes, Pumpkins (and Squash), Rocket, Salsify (and Scorzonera), Spinach, Tomatoes, Turnips* ***Fruit*** *Apples, late (Egremont Russet, Blenheim Orange, Orleans Reinette), Apples, store (Cox, Fiesta, Ashmead's Kernel, Bramley), Damsons, Grapes (English hothouse), Medlars, Pears, late (Concorde, Doyenne du Comice, Conference, Winter Nellis), Quince, Raspberries* ***Wild greens & herbs*** *Nettles, Watercress* ***Wild flowers & fruits*** *Bullace, Crab apples, Elderberries, Juniper berries, Rosehips, Rowan berries, Sloes* ***Fungi & nuts*** *Chanterelles, Chestnuts, Giant puffballs, Hedgehog fungi, Horse mushrooms, Oyster mushrooms (Pleurottes), Parasols, Shaggy ink caps, Summer truffles, Walnuts, Wood blewits* ***Fish & shellfish*** *Cod, Crabs (brown, hen and spider), Eels, Lobsters, Mackerel, Mussels, Oysters (native and rock), Prawns, Scallops, Sea bass, Sprats, Squid, River trout (brown and rainbow), Wild salmon* ***Game*** *Goose (wild), Grouse, Hare, Mallard, Partridge, Rabbit, Snipe, Grey squirrel, Wood pigeon*

Mushroom pâté

Heat *30g unsalted butter* in a large frying pan over a medium heat. Drop in *300g cleaned, trimmed and finely chopped mushrooms* and *4 finely chopped garlic cloves* and sauté, stirring frequently, for 10 minutes, or until all of the moisture in the mushrooms is released and has evaporated. Leave to cool for a few minutes. Blitz the mushrooms in a food processor until smooth, then add *250g cream cheese* and blitz again until well blended. Season to taste with *fine sea salt* and *freshly ground black pepper* and then leave to cool completely. Refrigerate for at least an hour for the garlic flavour to develop and serve in generous dollops on *crostini, or triangles of toast*. This pâté keeps very well in the fridge for up to a week. *Serves 6 as a starter.*

Pappardelle with ceps, sage and pancetta

Clean and trim around *750g ceps* and cut into thick slices. Heat *1 tbsp olive oil* in a large frying pan, add *150g finely diced pancetta or streaky bacon* and cook until well coloured. Add the ceps, *10 finely shredded sage leaves* (plus a few small leaves left whole), and *1 finely minced garlic clove*, stir well, and sauté for 4–5 minutes or until the mushrooms' liquid has evaporated and they're starting to colour. Season with *salt and black pepper* and turn off the heat but keep the mixture warm. Generously salt a large pan of boiling water and drop in about *400g fresh pappardelle pasta* and cook until al dente, a couple of minutes. Drain the pasta, tip it into the pan with the ceps and add *15g unsalted butter* and *1 tbsp olive oil*. Toss well and serve on warmed plates with *a grating or two of fresh Parmesan* if you like. *Serves 4.*

Breaded parasols

Make the mayonnaise by putting *1 free-range egg yolk*, *1 anchovy fillet*, *1 finely chopped garlic clove*, *½ tsp English mustard*, *a small pinch each of salt, sugar and black pepper* and *½ tbsp cider vinegar or lemon juice* into a food processor and blitzing until smooth. With the processor running, pour in *100ml olive oil* and *150ml groundnut oil* in a very thin trickle. As the mixture thickens, you can add the oils a little more quickly until you have a thick, glossy mayonnaise. Remove the stalks from about *400g parasol mushrooms* and clean the caps with a brush. Break the caps into generous bite-sized segments. Pour *groundnut oil* into a deep, heavy-based saucepan to a depth of 5cm and heat to 180°C, or until a cube of white bread dropped in turns golden brown in about a minute. Put *2 tbsp plain flour* in a small bowl and season with *salt and black pepper*. In a separate bowl, lightly beat *1 free-range egg*. Put *100g fairly fine, fresh white breadcrumbs* on a plate. Dust each mushroom with flour, dip in the egg and then in the breadcrumbs, making sure each piece is well coated. Drop a few at a time into the hot oil and fry for about 3 minutes until golden brown. Drain on kitchen paper and continue until all of the parasols are cooked. Serve immediately with the mayonnaise, *a sprinkling of flaky sea salt* and some *lemon wedges*. *Serves 6 as a starter.*

Pappardelle with ceps, sage and pancetta

Friday **2**

British Food Fortnight continues until Sunday 4 October

Saturday **3**

Sunday ○ **4**

Notes

October

5 Monday

6 Tuesday

7 Wednesday

8 Thursday

Friday **9**

Saturday **10**

Bridport Farmers' Market

Sunday ◑ **11**

Notes

October

12 Monday

13 Tuesday

14 Wednesday

15 Thursday

Friday **16**

Saturday **17**

Sunday ● **18**

Notes **October**

19 Monday

20 Tuesday

21 Wednesday

National Apple Day (commonground.org.uk)

22 Thursday

Friday

23

Saturday

24

Sunday

25

British Summertime ends (clocks back)

Notes

October

26 ◐ Monday

27 Tuesday

28 Wednesday

29 Thursday

November

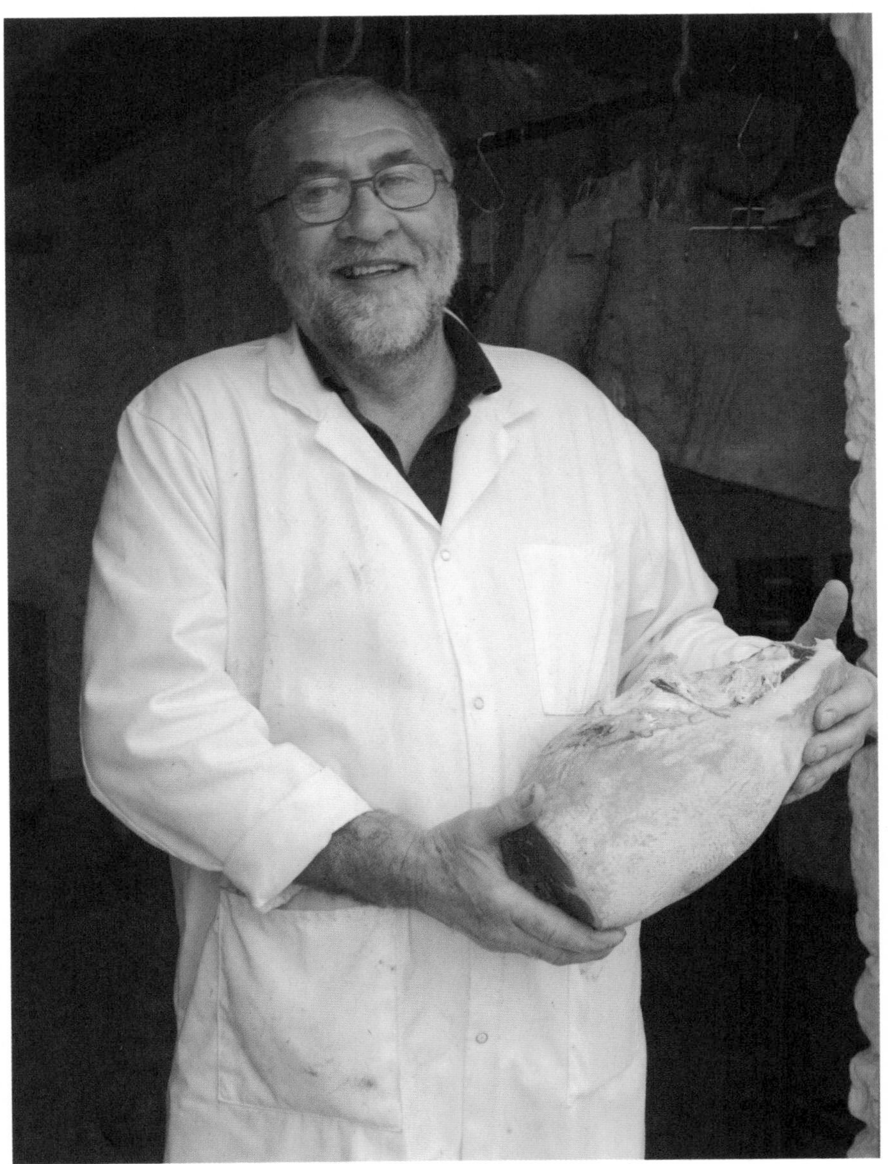

Curing and smoking
Ray Smith

Many of you will recognise Ray Smith, our butchery expert. He's been central to River Cottage's evolution since the beginning and his Curing and Smoking days are quickly booked up by those keen to bring home their own artisan-cured bacon.

Ray starts the day by presenting visitors with a whole side of pork, showing the location of each cured cut on the carcass – from boiled ham to streaky bacon. Then begins the fascinating business of curing and what Ray calls his 'Blue Peter bit', where he shows visitors pieces of meat which he's brined a day, a week and a month previously. 'It's all about watching closely and noting the changes,' he explains.

Next, Ray demonstrates everything from making dry-cured Parma-style ham to salami and venison biltong, before moving on to the difference between hot and cold smoking. Visitors end the day by tucking into Ray's delicious hot-smoked tenderloin and, he hopes, leave full of enthusiasm to try curing and smoking at home for themselves.

Getting started

— Start small and work your way up. Don't begin by experimenting with large and expensive cuts of meat – begin with salting a 2.5kg piece of belly pork until you feel confident enough to tackle a larger project.

— Teach yourself what to look for at each stage of the curing process by being observant – examine the meat regularly, don't just leave it and hope for the best.

— Hygiene is paramount when handling meat. Always make sure that all of your equipment and surfaces are immaculately clean.

Contacts

— For knives and mincing equipment try A.W. Smith: awsmith.co.uk.

— The Natural Casing Company sells sausage skins mail order: naturalcasingco.co.uk.

What's good in November

Vegetables *Jerusalem artichokes, Beetroots, Brussels tops, Cabbages (red, white and various green varieties), Cardoons, Carrots, Celeriac, Celery, Chard, Chicory, Endive, Greens (spring and winter), Kale (and Borecole), Kohlrabi, Leeks, Lettuces, Onions, Parsnips, Potatoes, Pumpkins (and Squash), Salsify (and Scorzonera), Swedes, Turnips* ***Fruits*** *Apples, late (Egremont Russet, Blenheim Orange, Orleans Reinette), Apples, store (Cox, Fiesta, Ashmead's Kernel, Bramley), Medlars, Pears, late (Concorde, Doyenne du Comice, Conference, Winter Nellis), Quince, Raspberries* ***Wild greens & herbs*** *Nettles, Watercress* ***Wild flowers & fruits*** *Rosehips, Sloes* ***Fungi & nuts*** *Chestnuts, Hedgehog fungi, Horse mushrooms, Oyster mushrooms (Pleurottes), Walnuts, Wood blewits* ***Fish & shellfish*** *Cod, Crabs (brown, hen), Lobsters, Mackerel, Mussels, Oysters (native and rock), Prawns, Scallops, Sea bass, Sprats, Squid, Whiting* ***Game*** *Goose (wild), Grouse, Hare, Mallard, Partridge, Pheasant, Rabbit, Snipe, Grey squirrel, Wood pigeon*

Dry-cured pancetta-style bacon

In a non-metallic container, thoroughly mix *500g salt*, *500g demerara sugar*, *4 finely chopped bay leaves*, *20 lightly crushed juniper berries* and *25g black pepper*. Put a thin layer of the mixture into the bottom of a large plastic container. Take a *2.5–3kg piece of pork belly*, bone in, and put it, skin side down, into the container. Rub a handful of cure into it. Cover and leave in a cool place for 24 hours. Remove the pork, pour off any liquid and rub it lightly again with the cure mixture. Repeat daily for 4–5 days. Wash all cure from the pork, clean it with a cloth soaked in *malt vinegar* and pat dry. Hang in a well-ventilated, cool, dry place for 7–10 days when it will be ready to use. You can keep the bacon hanging in a cool place or store it in the fridge for around a month. Take slices as you need them, removing the bones as you come to them.

Home-smoked pollack

Before cold smoking your fish, it needs to be salted. How much salt, and how long it takes, depends on the size of the *pollack*. For *small fillets and whole fish up to 500g*, scatter about *25g coarse sea salt* in a non-metallic container, lay the fish or fillet on it skin side down, then sprinkle another *25g coarse sea salt* over the top in an even layer. Leave for 15–25 minutes. For larger fish and *fillets up to 1.5kg*, use a total of about *75g coarse sea salt* and leave for 25–45 minutes. For *very large pieces, up to 3kg*, use about *110g coarse sea salt* and leave for 45–90 minutes. In all cases, wash off excess salt quickly but thoroughly under a cold tap and pat dry immediately before cold smoking. Once your fish is ready, you can use it in Cullen skink, kedgeree, fish pie and omelette Arnold Bennett.

Hot-smoked pork tenderloin

Combine *150g fine sea salt*, *4 shredded bay leaves*, *150g demerara sugar*, *1 tsp crushed juniper berries* and *1 tsp coarsely crushed black peppercorns*. Sprinkle half of the mixture into the bottom of a non-metallic bowl. Place *600g pork tenderloin* on top and scatter the rest of the cure mixture over it; gently massage it into the meat then allow it to sit for 30 minutes. Rinse the cure off the meat under a cold tap and dry on kitchen paper. Hot smoke the tenderloin over a gentle heat for 45 minutes. Check the meat temperature with a meat thermometer – it should read 70°C – and allow to rest before serving.

Dry-cured pancetta-style bacon

Friday **30**

Saturday **31**

Hallowe'en

Sunday **1**

Notes **_November_**

2 ○ Monday

3 Tuesday

4 Wednesday

5 Thursday

Bonfire Night

Friday **6**

Saturday **7**

Sunday **8**

Remembrance Sunday

Notes ***November***

9 ◑ Monday

10 Tuesday

11 Wednesday

12 Thursday

Friday **13**

Saturday **14**

Bridport Farmers' Market

Sunday **15**

Notes ***November***

16

● Monday

17

Tuesday

18

Wednesday

19

Thursday

Friday **20**

Saturday **21**

Sunday **22**

Notes ***November***

23 Monday

24 ◐ Tuesday

25 Wednesday

26 Thursday

Friday **27**

Saturday **28**

Sunday **29**

Notes ***November***

30 Monday

St Andrew's Day
Welsh Winter Fair (rwas.co.uk), until Tuesday 1 December

1 Tuesday

2 ○ Wednesday

3 Thursday

December

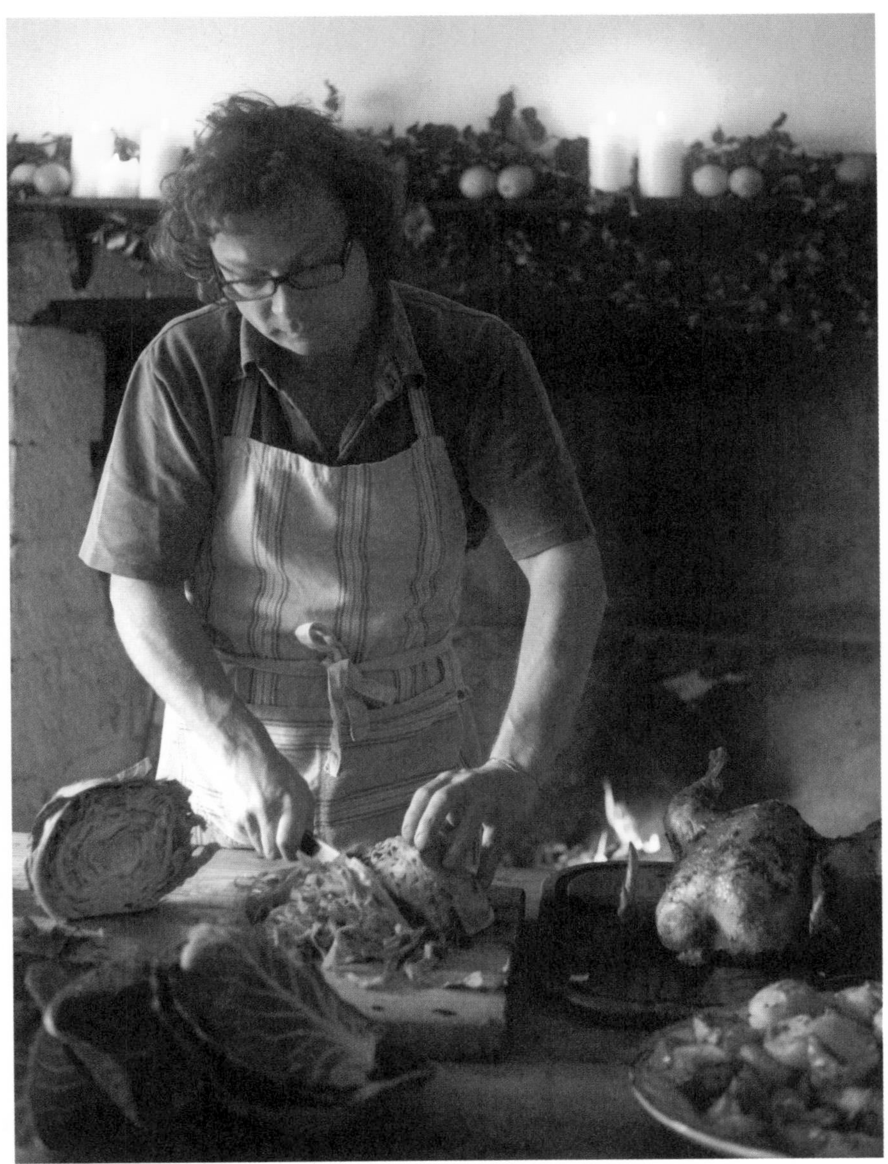

Hugh cooks Christmas
Hugh Fearnley-Whittingstall

At this most traditional time of year, many of us fall back into familiar patterns with barely a thought about whether or not we actually enjoy these long-held customs. Of course, we have a River Cottage antidote! Visitors to Hugh Cooks Christmas evenings are encouraged to leap out of that rut and take a fresh look at the most important meal of the year.

Don't like turkey? How about a forerib of beef, a great, free-range, organic chicken or goose, or even a baked bass or brill? For those of you with medieval aspirations and a houseful of mouths to feed, why not think about a multi-bird roast, an extravaganza of poultry and game, each bird stuffed inside a larger one?

As always with us, it's not just about the meat. Christmas Day should be celebratory, not an endurance test – either for the cook or the digestion – so Hugh presents some of his favourite festive vegetables in the form of zingy salads and canapés, as well as unusual side dishes for the main event.

And it wouldn't be Christmas without pud, would it? Our fresh look at the festivities includes a chocolate and chestnut cake and spiced, poached pears – destined, we hope, to become a new and delicious tradition in your family Christmas.

Getting started

— Don't be too hidebound by tradition. If you love fish or beef, make that the centrepiece of your feast.

— Don't forget your commitment to seasonality. It may bring some welcome surprises – celeriac, kale and salsify are all good now and make a great alternative to some of the usual Christmas veg.

— Get the kids involved making canapés, stuffing or pudding. Christmas is about sharing after all, and that includes sharing the work.

Contacts

— For free-range geese and turkeys, try Goodman's Geese, goodmansgeese.co.uk.

What's good in December

Vegetables *Jerusalem artichokes, Brussels sprouts, Brussels tops, Cabbages (red, white and various green varieties), Carrots, Celeriac, Celery, Chicory, Endive, Greens (spring and winter), Kale (and Borecole), Leeks, Lettuces, Onions, Parsnips, Potatoes, Swedes, Turnips* ***Fruit*** *Apples, late (Egremont Russet, Blenheim Orange, Orleans Reinette), Apples, store (Cox, Fiesta, Ashmead's Kernel, Bramley), Rhubarb (forced)* ***Fungi & nuts*** *Chestnuts* ***Fish & shellfish*** *Cod, Crabs (brown, hen), Mussels, Oysters (native and rock), Sea bass, Whiting* ***Game*** *Goose (farmed and wild), Grouse, Hare, Mallard, Partridge, Pheasant, Snipe, Grey squirrel, Woodcock, Wood pigeon*

Creamed Brussels sprouts with bacon

Trim *500g Brussels sprouts* and simmer gently in well-salted water for 8–10 minutes, until just tender. Drain, put in a food processor with *a knob of butter* and *2 tbsp double cream* and pulse several times until you have a rough, creamy purée. Cut up *4–6 thick rashers of streaky bacon* into 5–6 pieces each and fry them until crisp. Roughly chop or crumble about *250g cooked and peeled chestnuts*. In a medium-sized saucepan, stir the chestnut pieces into the creamed sprouts and gently heat through until thoroughly hot. Spread into a warmed dish and sprinkle over the crispy bacon bits. Serve at once, as a great accompaniment to goose, turkey or hot, glazed Christmas ham. *Serves 6.*

Chestnut, celery and liver stuffing

Preheat the oven to 180°C/Gas Mark 4. Over a medium heat, sweat *1 small, finely chopped onion* and *1 head of chopped celery* in *25g unsalted butter* for 10 minutes until softened. Add *12 plump, stoned and roughly chopped prunes*, *400g cooked, peeled and crumbled chestnuts* and *1 tbsp chopped parsley*. Season with *salt and black pepper* and cook for 3–4 minutes. Remove from the heat and cool slightly. Stir in *50g fresh breadcrumbs*, *1 trimmed, washed and finely chopped turkey liver* (optional) and *1 beaten free-range egg*, until well combined. Pile the mixture into an ovenproof dish and bake for 30–35 minutes until nicely browned and crisp on top. *Serves 8.*

Split pea and peppercorn purée

Soak *350g green split peas* overnight in plenty of cold water. Drain, rinse and put into a saucepan with *1 finely chopped onion*, *1 finely chopped carrot*, *1 finely chopped celery stick*, *1 small, chopped leek*, *a sprig of thyme* and *a bay leaf* and enough water to cover. Bring to the boil, then reduce to a simmer and cook until tender. Drain off the water, discard the bay leaf and thyme, and put the peas and vegetables, with *50g unsalted butter*, through a mouli-légumes, sieve or food processor (although the latter makes a less interesting texture). Now season to taste with *a pinch of caster sugar* and some *sea salt*. Add *1 tbsp drained, pickled green peppercorns* (preserved in brine, not dried) and mix well. Heat through before serving, thinning the purée with a little hot water if it is very stiff. *Serves 4, as a great accompaniment to rich meats such as roast goose.*

Split pea and peppercorn purée

Friday

4

Saturday

5

Sunday

6

Notes

December

7 Monday

8 Tuesday

9 ◑ Wednesday

10 Thursday

Friday **11**

Saturday **12**

Bridport Farmers' Market

Sunday **13**

Notes ***December***

14 Monday

15 Tuesday

16 ● Wednesday

17 Thursday

Friday **18**

Saturday **19**

Sunday **20**

Notes ***December***

21 Monday

Winter Solstice

22 Tuesday

23 Wednesday

24 ◐ Thursday

Friday **25**

Christmas Day (bank holiday)

Saturday **26**

Boxing Day

Sunday **27**

Notes

December

28 Monday

Bank Holiday

29 Tuesday

30 Wednesday

31 ○ Thursday

Friday **1**

New Year's Day (bank holiday)

Saturday **2**

Sunday **3**

Notes ***January***

Addresses

Name

Address

Telephone *Mobile*

Email

Name

Address

Telephone *Mobile*

Email

Name

Address

Telephone *Mobile*

Email

Name

Address

Telephone *Mobile*

Email

Name ....

Address ....

....

Telephone .... *Mobile* ....

Email ....

Name ....

Address ....

....

Telephone .... *Mobile* ....

Email ....

Name ....

Address ....

....

Telephone .... *Mobile* ....

Email ....

Name ....

Address ....

....

Telephone .... *Mobile* ....

Email ....

Name ....

Address ....

....

Telephone .... *Mobile* ....

Email ....

Name

Address

Telephone *Mobile*

Email

Name

Address

Telephone *Mobile*

Email

Name

Address

Telephone *Mobile*

Email

Name

Address

Telephone *Mobile*

Email

Name

Address

Telephone *Mobile*

Email

Name

Address

Telephone *Mobile*

Email

Name

Address

Telephone *Mobile*

Email

Name

Address

Telephone *Mobile*

Email

Name

Address

Telephone *Mobile*

Email

Name

Address

Telephone *Mobile*

Email

Name

Address

Telephone *Mobile*

Email

Name

Address

Telephone *Mobile*

Email

Name

Address

Telephone *Mobile*

Email

Name

Address

Telephone *Mobile*

Email

Name

Address

Telephone *Mobile*

Email

River Cottage HQ events & courses

At River Cottage HQ, we run a wide variety of events and courses in our cookery school and barn, plus bespoke events in our private farm house. Here is just a taster of what we have to offer …

Gardening (Season: April–November)
River Cottage Kitchen Garden takes visitors on a journey from plot to plate, exploring our gardens and polytunnels. Discover the art and science of sustainable gardening on our Green Kitchen Garden course or learn to make the most of every available square metre of space with the Urban Kitchen Garden day. Children will enjoy our Grab and Cook days (see May).

Bread making (Season: all year)
Join Aiden Chapman for a morning's bread making at his bakery in Lyme Regis then come over to River Cottage where Daniel Stevens, author of our *Bread Handbook*, will help you make the perfect loaf. Or join us for a Build and Bake day, where you'll learn how to build a clay oven and how to cook in one.

Preserving (Season: all year)
Our jam-making expert, Pam Corbin (see September), author of our *Preserves Handbook*, will show you how to create jams, pickles, syrups and curds from the best seasonal produce.

Evening events
Our evening event menus are based on the best local and seasonal ingredients, with each set menu uniquely devised by our head chef Gillon Meller (see January).

Join us for Friday or Saturday Night at River Cottage, or for one of our special celebrations throughout the year, including Hugh Cooks Christmas in December.

New courses for 2009
— An Introduction to Beekeeping
— Cheese and Yoghurt Making
— Pig Keeping

Go to rivercottage.net for a full list of events, courses and availability. You can also register to be kept informed of new dates via our Events pages as soon as we release them. All Hugh events and courses are released first to Members of River Cottage.

First published in Great Britain in 2008

Bloomsbury Publishing Plc, 36 Soho Square, London W1D 3QY
A CIP catalogue record for this book is available from the British Library.

ISBN 978 0 7475 8878 8

10 9 8 7 6 5 4 3 2 1

Design by Hyperkit

Photography by Gavin Kingcome except:
Cristian Barnett /Reproduced from Country Living/National Magazine Company/Retna UK: page 63 (April), page 101 (July). Colin Campbell: page 28 (Pot roast pheasant), page 40 (Eggy bread), page 52 (Apricot and honey flapjacks), page 66 (Kale and goats' cheese frittata), page 78 (New lettuce with 'soft' hard-boiled egg salad), page 92 (Potted shrimp), page 104 (Apricots on toast). Peter Higgins: page 9 (Pammy and Richie Riggs). Will Newbery: page 49 (March). Louis Quail: page 8 (Gillon Meller, Ray Smith, Daniel Stevens), page 12 (John Wright and Steven Lamb), page 151 (November).

Front and back cover photographs by Gavin Kingcome.

Printed and bound in Italy by Graphicom.

bloomsbury.com
rivercottage.net